TRANSFORM
THE ORDINARY

CAROLINE A. WESTERHOFF

Foreword by John H. Westerhoff

The Pilgrim Press
Cleveland

For
Betty and Terri
And always,
John

The Pilgrim Press, 700 Prospect Avenue East, Cleveland, Ohio 44115-1100
pilgrimpress.com
© 2001 Caroline A. Westerhoff

Westerhoff, Caroline A., 1940-
    Transforming the ordinary / Caroline A. Westerhoff; foreword by
John H. Westerhoff.
        p.   cm.
    Includes bibliographical references.
    ISBN 0-8298-1476-0 (pbk. : alk. paper)
    1. Meditations.   I. Title.

BV4832.3 .W48   2002
242—dc21

                                                         2002016956

Transforming the Ordinary

Contents

Foreword

Caroline Westerhoff is an accomplished author, lay canon in the Episcopal Church, and pastoral theologian. Her first two books, *Calling: A Song for the Baptized* and *Good Fences: The Boundaries of Hospitality* (Cambridge, Mass.: Cowley Publications, 1994, 1999, respectively), made significant contributions to our understanding of the Christian life of faith. Besides being a writer-theologian I admire and from whom I continue to learn, Caroline is my wife. She tells me that I am her toughest—and, therefore, most loving—critic. She claims to be grateful!

Storytelling has always been one of Caroline's greatest gifts, and in this current book, *Transforming the Ordinary*, she comes into her own. Through poignant, revelatory stories in the Wisdom Tradition, she helps us experience and understand the mysteries of God as a continuing process of unveilings—through nature, the arts, and our human lives.

To be human is to tell stories. We do so for many reasons: to inform or illustrate a conviction we hold; to attract attention, perhaps; or to entertain. Further, there are all sorts of stories: mythic legends told to establish some particular way to perceive life and our lives, historical narratives to explore perceptions and biographical accounts to test them, and parabolic tales intended to subvert how we presently discern reality so we might see it differently.

And then there are revelatory stories that tell of experience or observation, which, when reflected on, grant the possibility of new insight. Such accounts serve to unveil the heretofore hidden and make possible our receiving God's gift of wisdom. Typically, stories that support us in this quest for wisdom are tales of simple, ordinary occurrences presented in imaginative ways. They invite us to consider unasked questions, as well as provide the encouragement and help needed if we are to enter into new territory and come to new understandings—using both intuitive and intellectual ways of thinking and knowing.

Unfortunately, beginning with the Age of Reason in the seventeenth century, the intellectual way of thinking and knowing began to replace the intuitive. Logic replaced imagination, and theological reflection in the Wisdom Tradition fell into disregard—although never entirely. The English mathematician and philosopher Alfred North Whitehead, writing about inquiry into the nature of the universe, reminded us that tolerance for mystery is what invigorates the imagination and the imagination is what gives shape to it all. Indeed, August Kekule came up with the six-carbon ring structure when he envisioned the benzene molecule as a snake biting its tail while in whirling motion. The facts of organic chemistry known at the time could then fall into place.

Such giants in science have always appreciated that groundbreaking discoveries begin with an intuitive glimpse into the heart of the puzzle on which they are working. This glimpse must be filled in and expanded by reason, but without it, the breakthrough could not have occurred. Albert Einstein goes even further:

> The most beautiful experience we can have is the mysterious. It is the fundamental emotion which stands at the cradle of true art and true science. Whoever does not know it and can no longer wonder, no longer marvel, is as good as dead, and his eyes are dimmed. It was the experience of mystery—even if mixed with fear—that engendered religion. A knowledge of the existence of something we cannot penetrate, our perceptions of the profoundest reason and the most radiant beauty, which only in their most primitive forms are accessible to our minds—it is this knowledge and this emotion that constitute true religiosity. . . . [1]

We inheritors of an Enlightenment worldview too often continue making the intellectual way of thinking and knowing dominant, while depreciating the intuitive and placing the sciences over the arts. In doing so, we shut ourselves off from rich resources for revelation—

resources children still bring into play until we shake our heads in disapproval and show them otherwise. We need to consider that Jesus was being quite literal when he said we are to come to him as children come. Regretfully, we often ignore the child's gift of awe and wonder, the gift for which we pray at every baptism.

Learning how to perceive life and our lives and to live in faithfulness to these perceptions is ultimately of greatest worth. There is much we can discover if we keep our eyes open, if we are willing to be engaged by everyday experiences—our personal ones and those of others—and if we truly desire to strive—alone and with others—to learn from them.

In *Transforming the Ordinary,* Caroline encourages us to use the intuitive dimension of our lives and to engage our imaginations. She supports the development of our consciousness, that subjective awareness that makes particular experiences possible. And she invites us to catch our own glimpses of the mystery and recognize our own experiences of revelation—discoveries that have their source in scripture and tradition.

What now follow are a number of touching, engaging stories in the Wisdom Tradition. These stories can be read alone or in a group, aloud or in silence. Whatever the case, it is important that you take a time of silence afterwards to experience the story as yours. Then, once you have entered personally into it, reflect on your experience in the search for insights and implications for your life. If you do this in a group, you might describe your experiences, insights, and implications to one another. Opening and closing passages from the Psalms, as well as suggested questions to ponder and prayers to enliven and enlighten your own, can assist you in your meditations. I wish you well. A wonderful time lies ahead.

THE REV. DR. JOHN H. WESTERHOFF
Resident theologian and director of the
Institute for Pastoral Studies
St. Luke's Episcopal Church, Atlanta, Georgia

Acknowledgments

I find the acknowledgments page of a book difficult to write. Not because I think saying "thank you" is unimportant. Quite the contrary. Rather, I am aware that a host of voices—many of whom I could never name—influenced and informed me, and I would hate to leave anyone out. So I begin with thanks to all of them—whoever and wherever they are. I stand in their debt, more than I know.

Next come two who served as my readers along the way, Betty Barstow and Terri Tilley. They graciously delivered honest and insightful critique—when they did not need to squeeze anything else into their own jam-packed lives. They cheered and applauded—again, honestly I trust—when the muse took a break and I needed a lift. I will call on them again.

Deepest appreciation goes to Frank Allan, Sara Craig, Bob Hudak, Lee Harper Vason, Mary Lynn Owen, Elizabeth and Paul Murphy, and Giana Eden, who gave so generously of their time and placed their precious stories in my care. I hope I have been a faithful steward.

My colleague Linda Scott calmly took over the task of securing permissions for key quotations, getting me through a straw-and-camel's-back moment. I am fortunate that she is part of my staff team.

This is my first occasion to work with The Pilgrim Press. I have found Kim Sadler and Kathy Method not only highly competent but also considerate and kind, and I am sure they represent a host of others. I look forward to another time with them.

Finally, to my best friend and dear husband John, who understands the ups and downs of the writer's path better than anyone else I know: Thank you for all your encouragement—which includes tough words—and love and . . . good cooking! I am grateful that I walk into this always-uncharted territory with you at my side.

Preface

I marveled at her work, and the photographer allowed, "I seem to see what others often miss." She admittedly has an extraordinary eye, but I think the rest of us can make the same claim. We each have those moments when we catch glimpses of the mysteries of God—the holy clues God plants all around us—if we are but willing to recognize them. And as Paul writes to the Corinthians, we are to be trustworthy stewards of this holy evidence—to tell and show each other what we have heard and seen. Our challenge is this: to open the eyes of our hearts—to live expectant, epiphany-centered lives—so we can perceive and proclaim all that God is now ready to reveal. Living this way means that every day becomes a birthday with surprise packages to open and to prize as God continues to create.

These moments of revelation happen in a variety of ways. Ordinary encounters, perhaps, top the list: whether with a young man at a bus stop or a chipmunk in a cathedral's corridors. Then, there are memories of people and events long forgotten that somehow spring to life again, engaging us in webs of relationship and connection. Works of art—an old and beautiful plate; a mighty stone statue; a poem, play, dance, or symphonic score—provide windows into the riddle of our own being, as well as into the nature and intention of God. A fundamental purpose of art is, after all, revelatory—opening us to new possibilities—and our theologies were danced and sung long before they were written down and systematized. Robert Shaw, the late music director emeritus and conductor laureate of the Atlanta Symphony Orchestra and Chorus, went so far as to name art the "true transubstantiation . . . finally the Flesh become Word."[2]

I hope this collection of personal glimpses will encourage others to look afresh at their own everyday world—anticipating peeks into heaven and brushes up against God. I offer it as a quiet and sometimes playful guide into realms of reality unapproachable by sheer reason alone. Perhaps a park is the best analogy we have for the Reign of God.

When the imagination is playing its highest game, it is important not to let it come out into the open, lest reason should say "Nonsense" and the tension be lost.

—L. M. Boston, *A Stranger at Green Knowe*

A Dead Fish   1

O Lord, how manifold are your works!
In wisdom you have made them all;
the earth is full of your creatures.—Psalm 104

T HE YOUNG MAN STOOD OUTSIDE in the hall, anxiously wring-
ing his hands as he mustered the courage to knock. He had
made his way to Louis Agassiz's office at Harvard University and
then waited for what seemed an eternity before stepping up to
that fearsome door. The great nineteenth-century naturalist and
paleontologists answered the faint rap. He listened as his caller
blurted out a litany of admiration, closing with his heart's desire
to study in Agassiz's laboratory. To the student's amazement and
delight, his hero accepted him on the spot and gave him his first
assignment: to take a rather large fish—about a foot long—and
discover everything about it that he could.

Determined to please his mentor and carry out the most complete study ever done, he placed the fish on a laboratory dissecting
tray and launched into his task with fervor, making detailed notes
and drawings as he went along. He described the head, the torso,
the tail—eyes, fins, scales. He opened his specimen and began
carefully removing and preserving the gills and other organs in
vials of alcohol. He made notes and drawings regarding their func-
tions. Upon Dr. Agassiz's return many hours later, his pupil proudly
pointed to his accomplishment. The great one read his writings,
examined the precise drawings, and solemnly observed, "This is
impressive, but there is still more to do. I will be away for a period
of time. Please continue your work. I will look in on you when I
return."

The young man now began teasing out the fish's various muscles, pinning them to his tray and writing down descriptions of their movements. He removed the skull and the curving spinal column and arranged the many bones in neat rows. His notes and drawings were orderly and complete, and just as he sat back to draw a quick breath of satisfaction, Dr. Agassiz entered the laboratory again. He carefully went over his disciple's painstaking efforts and shook his head: "No, you do not yet have it." The student was at his wits' end. In exasperation, he exclaimed, "I can do no more. What else is there to know about a cold, dead fish?"

After a period of silence, Dr. Agassiz looked him straight in the eyes and passionately responded, "You have stated the problem for yourself. You never recognized and named the fish as a fellow creature. You did not pause before the mystery of its life and wonder about its story. Instead, you viewed that poor fish merely as an object to be taken apart and categorized piece by piece." He waited a few moments before continuing, now in a softer voice, "You indeed have much to learn."

My first reaction in the face of this delightful, years-ago story is to smile in smug appreciation of Dr. Agassiz's poetic wisdom. Silly student! How could he be so shallow? How could he stop so short of real comprehension? How could he presume the fish was only there to serve his need to impress? How could he think he would be able to know everything about it in the first place? Then, after this bit of self-righteous preening, I have the courtesy to wince, for the story sadly describes how we contemporary ones all too often see ourselves in relation to the natural order.

We believe that the purpose of nature is to serve us, to supply us with all we think we need. We carry out our letter-perfect dissections of anything and everything in our sway. We lay out bare bones on the tray, not worrying about putting them back together again. Bones are expendable. We sweep them away into the trash without a second thought. After all, we sit at the top of the heap, and it is our right to declare what is important and what is not. Granted, the heap is getting smaller, and we have inklings that there may not be enough of all it takes to keep us going unless we learn to manage our supplies a little better. But we trust that, finally, we have nothing to worry about. We are convinced that we can tackle the problem, dissect it, and figure it out. We believe that nothing lies beyond the scope of our mastery—a terrifying assertion, especially if it is true! The writer of Ecclesiasticus warns us not to meddle in matters that are beyond us, "for more than you can understand has been shown you."

How much more gracious and sane the way of Native Americans, who see themselves as beings among other beings. Beings who revere fish, deer, tree, and rock, aware that they are to respect and care for each of them. Beings who snare only what they need for survival and thank the one they kill for the precious gift of its life. What if we joined them and their kin and stood in awe before the secrets of nature? Suppose we bothered to listen for the voices and the stories humming in the air around us? What if we saw ourselves sitting in an even circle of friends, not in an elevated rank? Suppose we admitted that we will never know everything there is to know? Suppose we went a step further and said that we do not want to? Maybe we could then begin to call ourselves wise.

Yet, the fish story not only brings into question my relation to the natural order, it bids me to look at the way I address anything outside my own individualistic interests. How do I see my possessions and acquisitions? Am I free to do anything with them that I want? Is there any limit to what I can take over and secure for myself alone? Does anyone else have a legitimate claim to what I say is mine? How far can I go in defending what lies inside my domain? . . . Enough! Such deliberations disturb me. I prefer to avoid them. I am afraid I would not like my answers—if I dared be honest.

Still, the dead fish continues unrelentingly to examine me, now turning me toward my relationships with family and friends and colleagues. I wonder to what degree I am prone to dissect them, to lay out their bare bones—objects for my control and manipulation. I wonder why I resist recognizing that we can never know one another completely—that we are unfolding mysteries even to ourselves! And do I assume that once taken apart, I can put the dry bones back together again? Do I assume that I have the power to breathe into them so that, like Ezekiel's bones, they come to life and dance anew? Do I forget that the breath is not mine—but God's? With Dr. Agassiz's student, I seem not to see too far beyond the scope of my laboratory tray.

There is one more fish story to consider. I remember that Jesus fed the hungry crowd gathered before him on the hillside with a few dead fish and scant loaves of hard bread. He must have seen the people and the loaves and the fish as related to him and to each other in some mysterious way. We do not need to worry about how it happened. It did, and there was plenty. With God alone, all things are possible.

> Be still, and know that I am God!
> I am exalted among the nations,
> I am exalted in the earth.—Psalm 46

- What parts of God's world do I view as objects for my control or manipulation?
- What price will I pay if I treat them instead as honored companions in life?

◆ What graces will I need if I am to stop seeing myself as superior to the rest?

Creator God, you intend our dominion of creation to be marked by respect and mutual reliance. Grant us the will not to use or misuse any part of what you have placed in our care. Amen.

———

Be Perfect 2

The Lord will fulfill his purpose for me;
your steadfast love, O Lord, endures forever.
Do not forsake the work of your hands.—Psalm 138

THE BRILLIANTLY COLORED PLATE—blue, gold, green, white, reddish-orange—caught my eye and drew me to its case in a side gallery devoted to the favorite artifacts of the museum staff. The plate's intricate rim frames the central figure of a young woman clothed in Renaissance attire. She holds a stringed instrument and bow in her outspread hands and, behind her, a freestanding tree and the outline of a village complete the scene. But as charming as I found this piece to be, I could not miss its flaws. The edges of the rim were warped, and the entire painted surface bore visible cracks. It was far from perfect.

I leaned in closer to the case to read the small print on the identification card: "Artist unknown; Italy, 1530–1570; Tin-glaze earthenware." If the plate's vivid colors pulled me forward, the staff member's reason for selecting it captured my fancy. She chose the plate "for the mystery it holds regarding its very existence." She wonders why the artist did not just throw it away and start again when it became apparent his undertaking would not come out as he intended. "I like to imagine him perhaps fingering the rim of his damaged wares and deciding to go ahead and finish the work regardless," she writes. She muses about the generations who, down through hundreds of years, have used the plate to serve their food, valuing it and passing it from hand to hand, not minding its blemishes—at least not enough to discard it.

I showed a friend my photograph of the plate and asked, "Why was it kept all this time?" "Because it is beautiful!" she responded at once. Then, continuing, she added an unexpected twist: "I see the figure in the center as a musician who has just finished playing for her audience. Like the plate, performed music that is alive is always imperfect, never coldly correct. Neither the artist nor the audience knows how things will turn out at the beginning. That's the beauty of it." Her explanation carried an indictment of me. Not so far in the past, I might have discarded that plate because of the very flaws that render it lovely—just as over the years, I tossed away blemished shells picked up on early morning seaside walks. Only the perfect ones would do.

The struggle with perfectionism has long been my blessing and my curse. When I consider the blessing part, I grant that I am great with detail, the job gets done well, and I experience satisfaction—accompanied by applause to boot. The other side of the coin is that I can spend far too much time and energy on relatively unimportant matters—driving others and myself mad. I lose precious hours of sleep and become discouraged when I cannot meet my own impossible demands. But then the curse brings me back to blessing again. As I come to realize I cannot pull off even things that indeed matter, the applause takes on an increasingly hollow ring. As I realize I do not have time and energy to squander, I come to terms with what is significant to me. I take another look at Jesus' admonition: "Be perfect, therefore, as your heavenly Father is perfect."

Less and less do I now hear Jesus calling me into an absolute and hopelessly unattainable ideal—one without warp and crack. Rather, he calls me into wholeness—maturity, completeness. He calls me to be hospitable to those parts of myself that I reject and rule out. He invites me to realize my intrinsic beauty—enhanced by warp and crack! He says, "Be yourself—the one I love." Imagine that.

For many years, I have been drawn to "The Creation," the poem by James Weldon Johnson. However, before my love affair with the plate, I missed its point for me. In the earthy spirit of the old-time black preacher, Johnson presents God—after he puts the lights in the sky and fills the seas with fish and the woods with beasts and birds—as the lonely sculptor, squatting down and molding warm, wet river mud into fit company for himself:

> Up from the bed of the river
> God scooped the clay;
> And by the bank of the river
> He kneeled Him down;
> And there the great God Almighty
> Who lit the sun and fixed it in the sky,
> Who flung the stars to the most far corner of the night,
> Who rounded the earth in the middle of His hand;
> This Great God,
> Like a mammy bending over her baby,
> Kneeled down in the dust
> Toiling over a lump of clay
> Till He shaped it in His own image;
> Then into it He blew the breath of life,
> And man became a living soul.
> Amen. Amen.[3]

Johnson pictures God not as a cold, stiff monarch, sitting on his majestic throne, waving a rigid wand to bring us into being—and later brandishing it to keep us in line. Instead, he treats us to a figure with grimy hands, clay embedded under his fingernails, sleeves rolled up to his elbows, the knees of his pants stained by dark mud. God's streaked face reflects deep concentration as he shapes and reshapes his work of art—relishing an odd bump here and smiling over a little twist there. Then for his crowning touch, God brings the clay up to his mouth and bestows a wet kiss, breathing a great sigh of satisfaction as his handiwork wiggles and squirms into life. It is to his liking.

Is it possible that God enjoys us, not in spite of the bumps and lumps and twists, but because of them? because God finds us interesting in our eccentricities? because God's definition of worthiness is not limited by ours? because cold, stiff flawlessness does not fit so well with stained knees and a streaked face and dirt under the divine fingernails?

Artists I know who mold clay, paint on canvases, put words to paper, carve stone, and turn wood help me add another dimension to God the sculptor's work. They confess that when they attempt to impose their wills upon their work, disaster results. Clay becomes a hapless lump; colors lose their brilliance; words run together; sturdiest stones break into bits; wood cracks and splits. Rather, they describe a process of engaging their media, letting it determine the direction they will take. My friend Frank showed me the first wooden bowl he turned. He chuckled in chagrin as he pointed out seams of glue. "I tried too hard to get my masterpiece just right—to finish it," he admitted. "And it decided on its own to split apart—to say, 'I am as finished as I can be.'" Frank keeps the bowl to remind himself to let go.

In like fashion, God will not force us to be and do even according to the divine will. Our shaping and reshaping, complete with warp and crack, happen over the course of our lives—if we are open to receive the massaging of God's hands. I believe this is something of what Jesus means when he says to the hemorrhaging woman and to blind Bartimaeus, "Your faith—what I placed within you at the beginning—has made you well. You recognized and allowed it. Go forth in peace."

I sense that I am becoming more attuned to the God of the muddy riverbank these days—and to all those generations who treasured the beautiful plate and passed it along. A sign is that I gather seashells differently, now purposefully searching for the odd broken pieces, the old shells that are worn down and gnarled, laced with holes and crusted with barnacles. I look for the delicate spirals that are the ghostly remains of whelks and olives. I keep my eyes open for the labyrinthine remnants of moon shells and the smooth, tinged fragments that are gifts from the oysters. These are the ones that have lived interesting lives, that have ridden the waves and been tossed out on the beach, only to be swept up by rising tides for the wild spin all over again. The sand's polishing hand has not spared them. Their brushes and bumps up against each other have left their lovely thin-skinned countenances cracked and lined. Perhaps I see my own reflection in them. I layered a collection of these shells in a tall, clear-glass vase for my enjoyment.

> Let the favor of the Lord our God be upon us,
> and prosper for us the work of our hands—
> O prosper the work of our hands!—Psalm 90

- What parts of me can I see solely as warp and crack?
- What is the price I will pay if I accept and even come to appreciate them?
- What graces will I need if I am to affirm myself as whole and beautiful?

Artist God, like a potter you mold us into creatures you adore. Help us to embrace what appear to be flaws in our lives and to recognize the interior beauty that you already know and enjoy. Amen.

The Lord sets the prisoners free;
the Lord opens the eyes of the blind.—Psalm 146

S ARA, MY AROUND-THE-CORNER NEIGHBOR in Olde Ivy Square, had misplaced her keys—one more time. Frustrated, she made another clumsy turn around the back room of her town house, praying that she would get lucky and stumble upon them. Like many of us, Sara has played the challenging game of lost-and-found keys her whole life long. The added component these days is that she struggles with macular degeneration and cannot see so well. However, today's game of hide-and-seek had an unexpected dimension. Casting an inadvertent glance out the French doors opening onto her brick patio, Sara encountered our community's newest arrival. Etched on the oval scar on the trunk of an old maple tree—Sara requested the pruning to allow a little more light into her world— was a woman's face. Sara named her Our Lady of Olde Ivy and invited me over for an audience.

"Sit here for a good view." Sara motioned me to a blue leather chair behind a mahogany table filled with photographs and brochures from her latest trip abroad. Her gray and white cat Ashford hopped into my lap. "I do a lot of my work and eat my meals here," she said. "I call it my chair of vulnerability. I have raged and wept in it for months—as I cannot see the cowlick in the crown of my head or the keys on the kitchen counter or the cat's tail under my foot or the spot on my dress when I miss my mouth." She explained that depth perception is her worst problem. "Pouring anything can be a disaster," she warned as she served me a glass of red wine. "It often doesn't make it to the intended destination!" Her presentation this time went without a hitch.

"The loss of vision is more frustrating than my cancer ever has been," Sara confessed. She had a mastectomy in 1984, mere weeks after the death of her mother who lived with her at Olde Ivy. The disease recurred five years later, and she still visits her oncologist regularly. "I live my life in four-month increments. Let me put it this way: I don't buy green bananas!" Sara chuckled in her infectious manner. "I think I have dealt honestly with the cancer, and I never felt, 'Why me?' Rather, my question was, 'Why not me?' But this . . . this is a day by day, deed by deed, minute by minute thing, almost constant, and I have asked, 'Why me?' I am not afraid to die. I am only afraid of what kind of death it will be."

I sat in Sara's chair of vulnerability and gazed out the glass doors at the dark image of a face and neck cast on the scar's lighter background—rather like a one-dimensional cameo. A roll of bark draped over the top of the oval mark adds the likeness of a veil; a framework of bright green magnolia leaves, contributed by another floral resident of the garden, completes the setting. Our Lady gazed straight back at me. "From the chair, she is right in the line of vision of my remaining good eye, and in the softer light of the late afternoon or the early morning, she is even clearer," Sara told me. "It was a while before I saw her upstairs. She just appeared one evening—reflecting the patio floodlight, framed by the bedroom shutters." Sara hesitated and continued, "I call her Our Lady, but I don't have to believe that she is the Virgin Mary or my mother or even a guardian angel. What I know is that God placed her before me and I believe, for a purpose. It's as if . . . as my sight dims, I can see more, and in the seeing, I regain the serenity—the healing—that has eluded me." Sara repeated for me the litany she hears God whisper in her ear every day:

You have sat in this chair and wept for months.
Now I have given you something you can see—
     even your camera can see it!
This picture is also on your heart.
And when you see her, you see me,
     because I put her there.
She is my handiwork.
I do not need Michelangelo to do my painting;
     I paint too.
Even if your days become dark tomorrow,
     you will have seen me.
You will know that I am with you until the end of time.

A mutual friend chided me, "Don't encourage her. She's really getting carried away with this 'Our Lady' business. It's not like Sara." As Sara herself says, "I am a very practical person—not someone given to odd experiences. I wasn't looking for her—I was looking for my keys!" A staunch Democrat, she has always been involved in politics, even working for a prominent Georgia congressman in Washington. For many years, she served as regional director of the Department of Health and Human Services in Atlanta, and after she retired, the Centers for Disease Control and Prevention asked her to return as one of its writers. Soon to turn eighty, Sara—in the company of assorted friends—continues to embark on exotic trips abroad: Russia . . . Greece . . . Hungary . . . Saudi Arabia. Most recently, she set off on a barge trip down the Rhine Canal in Alsace. Reports have it that Sara held court every afternoon. And upon her return, she up and joined a group from her parish who regularly read the service of Compline with women held in Atlanta's City Jail—"to give them a chance for some serenity," she explained. Her one concern: Would there be illumination enough for her to see the print? "Don't worry, Sara; we'll take our own floodlight!"

At the end of the day, Sara is first and foremost a daughter of the church. So right after she assures me that she is a practical person, not given to odd experiences, she adds, "But our faith involves a lot of mystery and, to some I'm sure, rather strange goings-on. Given all the rest of it, I guess the likeness of a woman on a tree trunk in my backyard is pretty tame stuff!" She then proceeds with her own affirmation: "I believe . . . that God sees after us and gives us a push here and there to help us through whatever circumstances we find ourselves in—including those scrapes we conceive on our own." Defiantly, "It doesn't matter to me whether anyone else sees Our Lady or not. She is my push. Many years ago, I struck the word 'coincidence' from my vocabulary. 'Faith' works better."

Sara brings her faith—what she sees—to everything else she sees, and this faith makes it possible for her to see even more. In turn, this "even more" points her toward renewed faith: seeing through the eyes of God. Sara would simply say that faith is sight, and sight proceeds to heightened faith. Round and round, over and over, ever and ever. My thoughts fly to the lyrical opening of the eleventh chapter of Hebrews: "Now faith is the assurance of things hoped for, the conviction of things not seen. . . . By faith we understand that the worlds were prepared by the word of God, so that what is seen was made from things that are not visible."

Perhaps Sara's understanding of faith helps explain why Jesus so often appears to concern himself with blindness and sight— things unseen and seen—turning it all upside down and leaving us dizzy as we try to perceive who sees and who does not. Perhaps her understanding of faith is what moves us to the communion table, our hands stuck out for the bread and the wine that we say are also the body and blood of Christ. Why else would we find ourselves performing such an improbable act? And why would we return again and again if something did not happen to us and within us at the altar rail? The whole business reminds me of the conundrum of the chicken or the egg: Which comes first—faith required or faith received? The answer for me has always been, "It doesn't matter." You simply have to start with the one you see on your doorstep.

Sara stopped by my office a few days after my audience before Our Lady and thrust several sheets of paper across my desk. "About a year ago, I wrote this in the middle of the night from the depths of my despair—before she appeared," Sara confessed. "I'd like you to have it. Everyone hasn't listened to me."

Why?

The rich dark brown in a painting by Vermeer;
The early morning light on the lagoon in Venice;
The soaring high altar of Canterbury Cathedral;
The slow, precise descent of the Met's chandeliers;
The face of Leonardo's angel in "The Annunciation";
The perfectly framed small piece of Tuscany,
      seen through the lens of a camera;
The stark white of the Acropolis,
      against the deep blue of sky and sea; . . .
San Francisco Bay at night,
      seen from a slowly descending airliner;
The eerie light of a summer midnight in Norway;
The spidery old script proclaiming,
      "We the people of the United States";
 The word "Byzantium,"
      which looks and sounds like what it is; . . .

Never to see these things again?
Why?
That I might better see the need in the voice of a friend—
    or stranger.
Why?
That I might better see the care in the faces
    looking back to see if I'm all right.
Why?
That I might better see the stolen Bellini "Madonna,"
    in the empty frame that hangs in a Venetian church.
Why?
That I might better see the apples on the trees in Normandy,
    when I taste a sip of Calvados.
Why?
That I might better see the victory of the human spirit,
    when I hear someone . . . sing "Nessun Dorma." . . .
Why?
That I might better see the silent trust of my cat Ashford,
    as she sits beside an empty plate and looks up at me; . . .
Why?
That I might better see in the midst of rain,
    the clearing heaven's hue.
Why, God?
Is it that I might better see You?

Sara hesitated at the door and glanced back over her shoulder—her cockeyed cowlick at its best worst. Giving me a puckish grin, she chuckled—counseled—"Don't forget; you saw her too!" I guess I had better look for my chair of vulnerability.

> For with you is the fountain of life;
> in your light we see light.—Psalm 36

- What is the blindness that makes it difficult for me to see God in my life?
- What price will I pay if I am healed of my blindness?
- What graces will I need if I am to accept God's healing power?

Ever-healing God, you give sight to the blind.
Open our eyes so we might see more clearly
your tender presence in our lives. Amen.

———

Adventure   4

The Lord is my light and my salvation;
   whom shall I fear?
The Lord is the stronghold of my life;
   of whom shall I be afraid?—Psalm 27

THE YOUNG BLACK MAN IN JEANS and a windbreaker settled
sideways on the green wooden bench at the bus stop. He swung
his feet down and moved over to make room when I arrived. We sat
together a short while before he looked up from his book to begin
the pleasantries of stranger-to-stranger conversation in the South.
"It's a nice morning," he opened.

"Couldn't be better," I agreed.

"You going to church?" he inquired. I nodded. "Me too," he said,
and we swapped the names of our respective destinations. He then
stuck out his hand and volunteered, "I'm Bobby."

"I'm Caroline," I allowed, offering mine in return.

"That's with an '-ine,'" he declared. "I know the difference. My
mother is Carolyn, and my sister is Carol. I don't get them mixed up."
I smiled, so pleased that my new friend heard my often-mispronounced
name correctly.

Bobby held up a tattered paperback copy of Norman Vincent
Peale's *The Power of Positive Thinking* and asked, "You ever read this?
It's a great book," he continued before I could answer. "A teacher
gave it to me when I was in the eleventh grade in 1983. I have to
keep reading it so I won't lose what it says." I nodded, and he went
on, "It says that change only starts inside you. Trying to change
other people won't work. And besides, it's not right." I nodded again,
this time having the courtesy to blush. Bobby had inadvertently

delivered a well-placed jab smack on my bent to ignore too often the log in my own eye. His timing was perfect: only minutes before I was to pray the words of confession—once more so I won't lose what they say.

My companion was on a roll of self-revelation. "I'm a positive rapper," came next.

"I like rap," I responded, making an emphatic, circular movement with my hand and arm, bobbing my head to a steady if silent beat.

He gave me a look of, "You gotta be kidding," and blurted out, "That blows me away!"

"Why?" I asked.

"'Cause most older white women don't know what rap is—much less claim to like it." I sniffed but said nothing. Older white woman was not exactly how I would have described myself, all dressed up that lovely Sunday morning. Still in retrospect, I decided that being an older white woman—particularly one who likes rap—might not be such a bad thing. Maybe it's even pretty cool. I just had never thought of myself that way before. "I also make prophecies," Bobby owned. "The coming of the Lord will be very soon now. We're going to have to be ready." Something else to think about. When our bus arrived, he motioned me on first and then went far to the back to continue his reading.

I take public transportation to church every Sunday in order to come home with my husband John at the end of his long morning as a priest at Saint Luke's. Or so it began. I walk three blocks from my front door to the bus stop at the corner of Piedmont and Habersham Roads, ride bus number five to the Lindbergh Station several miles farther, and catch a southbound train to the Civic Center Station, three blocks from Saint Luke's. The entire trip takes close to forty minutes. I have friends who consider my Sunday morning junkets silly—"The drive home alone wouldn't be that long!"—or dangerous—"Isn't the Civic Center Station awfully deserted?"

"Yes, but I move quickly through, eyes straight ahead," I assure them.

Several lonely alley and parking lot entrances punctuate my walk from the station to the church, and I admit they evoke an occasional anxious twinge as I approach and pass them. However, for the most part, I am not afraid. I enjoy being out there. Who knows what modest adventure—like finding Bobby at the bus stop—might be in store? Along the way, I meet a few homeless men from the nearby shelter, bags of belongings slung over their shoulders. They frequently speak before I can murmur, "Good morning." An old man sitting on the alley wall greeted me with, "You're such a pretty lady," as I went by. Head up, I sailed into church and then into the week ahead on the strength of his salute.

The late Rabbi Edwin Friedman says that seeking adventure before safety—doing new things in new places with new people—is what it takes to free the imagination so we can see new possibilities and disentangle ourselves from old patterns. Adventures spin us around and point us in new directions. They knock us off our familiar props and disorient us so we can ask new questions and make new connections. Friedman adds that failure of nerve is the danger we should fear most, for reorientation can be precarious business. It means the unexpected and unanticipated—what we do not control—become the order of the day.

With his subversive stories and his custom of connecting with all kinds of unlikely people, Jesus also seems to prize disorientation and new direction. My suspicion is that not only does Jesus intend to unsettle those he meets, but he also seeks his own fresh bearings in their exchanges. "Sir, even the dogs under the table eat the children's crumbs," the Canaanite woman challenges. Jesus hears. He heals her stricken daughter. He alters his primary course in pursuit of the Jewish people, now responding as well to faith found in strange corners.

I picture God cheering us on when we scrape up enough courage to get out there and encounter those outside our usual circle of friends—those we are not apt to invite to dinner and who are not apt to invite us either. Isaiah puts it something like this: Go ahead, and catch a glimpse of God's new thing that even now is springing forth and breaking from the bud! Indeed, our willingness to head off—to go somewhere—is, at the end, the only part of adventure we can manage on our own. We cannot draw the map. We cannot orchestrate our encounters or carry scripts in our hands. Even with books about positive thinking and missals chock-full of prayers tucked securely under our arms, we cannot determine what will or will not come to pass. And I believe this is a good thing. My limited imagination could not possibly dream up the marvels in store as the divine itinerary rolls on ahead of me. W. H. Auden writes:

> He is the Way.
> Follow Him through the Land of Unlikeness;
> You will see rare beasts, and have unique
>   adventures.
>
> He is the Truth.
> Seek Him in the Kingdom of Anxiety;
> You will come to a great city that has expected
>   your return for years.
>
> He is the Life.
> Love Him in the World of the Flesh;
> And at your marriage all its occasions shall
>   dance for joy.[4]

Perhaps Bobby and I caught a glimpse of God's celebration that morning, where companions dance for joy, where Isaac and Ishmael realize that they are both flesh of Abraham—more alike than all that different.

And so it continues every week. I make my way by foot, bus, and train and take my place in the pew, ever hopeful that . . . who knows? Perhaps this is the day that I will be surprised or tipped off balance. Yet, more Sundays than not, I wait alone on the green wooden bench, and no old man greets me with words of ovation as I walk up the street. The only further occasion I saw Bobby, he asked, "We've met before, haven't we? You're . . . you're . . . Carolyn." I nodded at him in amusement as he joined my other friends who just cannot get it right.

> He put a new song in my mouth,
> a song of praise to our God.—Psalm 40

- From what safe place in my life do I need to venture forth?
- What price will I pay if I risk moving away from safety and security?
- What graces will I need if I am to find the courage to do so?

Pilgrim God, you call us to trust you in our pilgrimage of life. Grant us the confidence to step out into the unknown so you might surprise us anew. Amen.

———

Creatures Great and Small   5

 He brought me out into a broad place;
   he delivered me, because he delighted in me.—Psalm 18

OUR SPRAWLING CATHEDRAL PRESENTS visitor and denizen alike with a convoluted maze of doorways and stairwells that connect floors of hallways running at angles to each other. I have worked here off and on for nearly twenty-five years, but on any given day, I still need to stop and figure out exactly where I am and how I am going to reach my desired destination.

On one particularly lovely Saturday afternoon in April, as I made my way to my bottom-floor office to pick up needed materials for a workshop, a chipmunk shot out right under my feet. He scurried away and disappeared around a corner. Hoping I could direct him to an exit door and safety, I followed his progress through several interconnecting corridors and rooms—the workshop wiped from my mind. The little guy offered a measure of cooperation by pausing under and behind anything and everything in his path, allowing me to catch up before he took off again.

He finally settled under a piano in a large space where an out-of-town youth group had spread their sleeping bags for the weekend's stay. I closed the heavy entrance doors and went back to my office to make a sign enlisting their aid: "CAUTION— CHIPMUNK!! HELP HIM GET OUTSIDE!!" Taping it up in plain view, I walked on through the room into a short corridor and stairwell containing stacks of gray plastic storage bins. Here, I caught a glimpse of my furry friend again. He had dashed on ahead of me, darting behind the containers. I doubled back, closed off the youth room, and inhaled that sweet smell of success. There were doors leading to his freedom at the top of the stairs! Certainly, I could work him up and out.

The chipmunk and I then began a slapstick dance that would have made Laurel and Hardy proud. I rattled the bins. He ran out and started up the stairs. I followed, urging him along with a broom I found in a corner of the stairwell. He countered with a quick about-face, scooted back down the stairs, hid again, and we began our frenetic ritual one more time. I do not know how many trips we made, but before long, I was exhausted and discouraged. I had to admit that my strategy was flawed and I needed an ally to cut Mr. Chipmunk off and keep him moving toward the exit doors. But, unfortunately, he and I seemed to have this part of the building to ourselves.

Terrified that I would lose him, I raced up to the reception area outside the Hall of Bishops on the next floor and, to my relief, saw a potential partner—of sorts. Standing in the empty hallway reading a bulletin board was an unassuming little middle-aged man dressed in khaki shorts and a beige T-shirt, a nondescript leather bag slung over his shoulder. He wore thick glasses, sensible brown walking shoes, and a narrow-brimmed khaki canvas hat with a braided cord passing under his chin—cowboy style. "TOM" was printed in bold letters on the piece of silver duct tape stuck to the right side of his shirt. While not terribly impressive, he was all I had, and he would have to do. "Tom," I began, "could you help me for a few minutes?" As matter-of-factly as I could muster, I went on, "I am trying to rescue a chipmunk caught in this building." My new comrade did not seem to think my request the least bit odd and nodded his solemn assent.

I led him back through the hall to the stairwell, grabbing up a deep tray as we passed the kitchen door. "Perhaps we can catch him in this and take him outside," I suggested. We went down the stairs, and I rattled the storage bins, letting out a sigh of relief when my little friend scampered forth. The sight of the chipmunk transformed Tom into a crusading knight. He seized the tray from my hand, and man and beast began their own up-and-down dance. I took my place at the top, ready to prevent the chipmunk's streaking off into the Hall of Bishops rather than heading outside. The stairs turned a corner at a landing, so I could not see what was going on at the bottom. But I could hear, and the noise was loud and frightening as Tom shook the bins and made lunge after lunge at the tiny creature with the container. I began to worry about his safety in a new way: Suppose Tom killed him or broke his back? Suddenly, there was silence.

I held my breath as Tom rounded the landing corner in triumph, holding the vessel out before him like a priceless offering. I glanced inside and saw the little guy frozen in terror in a corner. He seemed to be all right. Tom glided past me out the door without a word. I watched as he crossed to the middle of the lawn, stopped by a large tree, knelt down, and turned the tray on its side. He waited as the chipmunk presumably ran off—I could not see what was happening—then rose and moved back to me. "Tom, you're a hero!" I cried.

"At least to a chipmunk," he returned with an aw-shucks shrug. I had the feeling he had never been called a hero before, and I hoped it would not be the last time. We all need someone who believes we are noble. Without a word, Tom handed the container to me. We acknowledged each other with a slight bow and parted company. I never learned who Tom was or where he came from, but maybe real heroes are like that.

On my way back to the neglected workshop, I went all through the cathedral, closing as many outside doors as I could, hoping to ward off another small one's straying inside. Before I went home,

I walked out to the tree, praying I would not find a stiff little body—even though I would have preferred his dying outside in the grass rather than within the alien confines of the building. I was aware of the tightness in my chest. There was no trace of him. I exhaled.

A colleague who does not even pretend to be an animal lover later added more detail to the chipmunk's journey to freedom. To her horror, she chanced upon him even before I did and beat a hasty retreat behind a slammed-shut office door. Coupling her account with mine, I became aware of the rather amazing course he took through the labyrinthine hallways in a very short period of time. He always appeared to be moving toward a way out of the building—toward fresh air and the light. It was as if an internal guiding mechanism were built right into him. But doesn't that seem like the way a kind and meticulous Creator would design things? And once said, the leap is not too great to suppose that we have a guiding compass built into us as well, one on which we can rely—ofttimes with the help of our friends—as we work our way toward fresh air and the light. I think it is what some call intuition or, perhaps, a sixth sense. I reckon it grace.

I imagine there are those who will deem this story silly, not worth the writing, who will say that Tom and I were foolish to devote so much time and energy to the rescue of an inconsequential and pesky rodent. What harm, they will ask, would have been done if he had died in the bowels of the cathedral—other than a fleeting foul odor? Why did we bother? But such thinking raises a different sort of quandary for me: Why does God bother? What if God calculates our significance only as the mere specks in the universe that we in truth are? What if God does not think our story worth the telling or the trouble to turn it around? Who are we—who are but dust, whose days are like the grass—to know the sweep of God's concern? God asks Job, "Where were you when I laid the foundation of the earth? Tell me, if you have understanding." I bow my head before the question.

> What are human beings that you are mindful of them,
> mortals that you care for them?—Psalm 8

- What part of me wonders if God really cares?
- What price will I pay if I come to accept God's sweeping love?
- What graces will I need if I am to believe that God deems me precious?

Ever-loving God, you have made us for yourself, and our hearts are empty without you. Draw us closer to you that we might love ourselves as much as you love every part of who we are. Amen.

———

Marked

6

He sent signs and wonders into your midst,
O Egypt.—Psalm 135

N ANCY'S JOB AS A CONSULTANT to churches takes her all over the country. She delights in regaling her friends with accounts of the triumphs and tragedies that are ever the lot of the frequent flyer, and we enjoy her tales. "You won't believe what happened!" she starts, and we sit back, anticipating another high-spirited spin involving elevators, taxis, and what have you. This day however, her mood is different: a subdued and pensive Nancy sits across the lunch table from me. "My last trip to New York left me unsettled," she begins after a while, flicking lettuce leaves around her plate, "and I'm not sure why. I had a series of encounters with other travelers on my way there and back. None was very dramatic, but I can't get the accumulation of them out of my mind." With a nod, I encourage her to go ahead, and she launches into her story.

"Right off the bat, a man with a sleepy blond child in tow stopped me on Atlanta's B concourse as I headed off toward my early-morning gate. He asked if they were going in the right direction to the terminal. I answered yes, smiling sympathetically as I remembered times when I had my own sleepy blond children in tow. That was all there was to it. However, the concourse was crowded even at this unholy hour, and I was aware that he had stepped out of his way, cutting across a stream of human traffic to come to me.

"Believe it or not, a woman speaking in rapid and unbroken Spanish, arms flailing the air, eyes flashing, stopped me once more before I reached my destination. I don't speak Spanish, and I never knew exactly what her problem was. But I am good at arm waving, too, and I managed to maneuver her to an information desk before continuing on.

"Finally on the plane and determined to claim some peace and quiet prior to the day's round of meetings, I conspicuously buried myself in a mystery book. I soon discovered that peace and quiet were not to be. My seatmate was a young woman traveling from the island of Martinique to the United States. Hair neatly plaited, eyes enormous and dark, she was determined to talk, and she won. I found I could still handle a little college French (*Je m'appelle . . . mais oui . . . s'il vous plaît . . . escargot . . . bientôt . . . alors!*). For her part, my companion could contribute a smidgen of English to our stumbling communication—efforts that regularly reduced us to fits of girlish giggling. She had many questions about New York and the United States, and I did my best with them. On the other hand, she never gave a clue about the nature of her trip. Now determined to deliver my new charge to someone after we left the plane, I was both relieved and surprised when the 'someones' turned out to be two Roman Catholic nuns. She bid me good-bye with a tilt of her head. I replied with a thumbs-up gesture of encouragement—for whatever lay ahead.

"There was yet more. The inevitable announcement of delayed flights came over the loudspeaker when I arrived back at LaGuardia late that afternoon. No sooner had I settled in for the long wait—mystery book in one hand and a large cup of coffee in the other—than a distinguished, older African American woman came over from across the room. She dropped down next to me, ticket in hand. Not a usual traveler by air, she was uncertain about the significance of the delay. I checked her ticket and reassured her, translating 'airplane' for 'equipment.' She thanked me graciously, wished me a good flight, and returned to her own seat and book."

At the conclusion of her story, Nancy asks, "Why me? I felt like a marked woman—like I was sitting under a blinking neon light: 'Ask me; ask me anything! I specialize in palms and tarot cards!'" We laugh, but her question is serious: "Why me?"

I shrug, "You must look like you know what you're doing."

"I don't think I look that supremely confident out there," she protests. "Traveling always keeps me a little off center."

"Maybe it was just your day for duty in traffic control," I quip, and we move on to something else. Nancy finishes her salad.

I now take my turn playing over and over the events of her day—especially her words before we changed the subject: "I felt like a marked woman." The ominous prophecy of the old Western movie first comes to mind: He is a marked man—designated for death—not long for this world! But next, my memory flicks through the use God makes of marks in the biblical record—the protective one given the murderer Cain, signifying the always-overriding rule of divine mercy; the one placed on the foreheads of the righteous of doomed Jerusalem by Ezekiel's mysterious man in linen; those conferred to differentiate God's servants and the worshipers of the beast, before Revelation's tumultuous events play out and the new Jerusalem descends from heaven in her glory. They all point to God's will—to be done on earth as it is in heaven. And then, I come to the brands and seals and marks in Galatians and Ephesians and in my Episcopal prayer book's baptismal rite: You are sealed by the Holy Spirit in Baptism and marked as Christ's own forever. You are a marked woman. From this day forward, you will bear the brand of Jesus.

A little sheepishly, I go to the mirror and scrutinize my reflection, but I find no glistening trademark on my forehead indicating divine connections or bestowing special status. I do see the delicate gold cross I wear around my neck every day—unless conscious of fashion, I change to the silver one to coordinate with other pieces of jewelry. But I suspect I too often deem it as much a good luck charm as a proclamation of radical identity. And I suspect the collars worn by my ordained sisters and brothers can too often be the same for them. After all, the visible collar has more than once prevented a speeding driver from collecting a traffic ticket—or paying full freight for a variety of affordable services.

So I move on to the possibility that our real God-marks are ones that only others can see. Maybe they are like the lemon juice letters we children scrawled on paper to preserve and pass along our secret messages—letters that become visible only when a hot iron is applied. Maybe Christ-brands only show when someone needs a hot touch from God. I remember how, after the resurrection, Jesus invites Thomas to reach inside him—into his wounds—so Thomas can believe. But Thomas does not have to. The invitation is enough. The heat of the moment is searing, and the words issue forth—"My Lord and my God!"

I then wonder about times when those others may have seen my mark and chosen me, and I did not know it. I wonder if I came through with what they were seeking. More important than the gold cross or the clerical collar is the answer to the question: Does its bearer finally deliver the goods of good news? At last, with the mirror's help, I look into my eyes and remember that Jesus calls them the lamp of the body—the mirror of the soul. If your eye is healthy, your whole body is full of light. If it is not healthy, your body is full of darkness.

In that flash, I recognize that the seal of God is not a brand crudely fixed on our external parts. Rather, its graceful lines are set deep within us. Like sticks rubbed together, they spark the fire and ignite the lamps of our souls. And when we are at our best, we serve as holy icons, into and through which the beholder can see those illuminated wounds of pure love. May our eyes shine with the truth of who and whose we are. May they be bright beacon lights for weary and confused travelers, making their way through regions that can be dark indeed.

> You make the winds your messengers,
>   fire and flame your ministers.—Psalm 104

- How has God marked me to be a sign of divine presence in the world?
- What price will I pay if I acknowledge and manifest that sign?
- What graces will I need if I am to be faithful to my marking?

Summoning God, you sealed and marked us at baptism to be your holy heralds. Grant us the insight and the passion to make your light shine for all whom we meet. Amen.

Holy Family

7

For I am but a sojourner with you,
    a wayfarer, as all my forebears were.—Psalm 39 (BCP)

B OB, A SPIRITED PRIEST IN HIS middle fifties, drove up to his storefront church and looked in the window of the unfamiliar, dilapidated truck parked in front. An old man with sunken cheeks and thin gray hair slept at the wheel. Bob went on inside the building and instructed the parishioner answering the phone that morning, "Please call me when he wakes up. He's going to need help." A short time later, the stranger pulled open the door and presented himself at the reception desk, and as Bob made his way toward him across the space that was nave, parish hall, and meeting room all rolled into one, the man spoke his name—"Bob. . . ." In the flash of an instant, Bob saw the face of a fourteen-year-old classmate in Saint Joseph's Seraphic Seminary, the Franciscan boarding school they both attended some thirty-seven years before. "I don't think I would recognize myself at that age," Bob admitted to me later, "but I immediately knew he was George."

The two boys had not been close friends back then; George, in fact, graduated from another school. While each eventually became a Franciscan, George chose not to be ordained and remained a brother. A brilliant man, he worked among the homeless and was a college professor before leaving the order in 1988. "I think the last time our paths crossed was about 1974," Bob recalled. "The strongest tie we probably ever had was at Saint Joseph's, when we walked around the lake after supper and one of the upperclassmen led the Franciscan Crown." I gave him my best look of incomprehension, and he explained, "That's the seven-decade rosary extolling the Seven Joys of Mary. The twilight prayer was a school custom, and the Crown remains part of my prayer life even today." Bob reflected, "At first, I thought it was the spirit of Francis, hovering over us, that brought George and me together after all those years. But lately, I have begun thinking that Mary might be the connection—that all along, George was joining me in praying to God through her prayer—"

> Hail Mary, full of grace,
> the Lord is with you!
> Blessed are you among women,
> and blessed is the fruit of your womb, Jesus.
>
> Holy Mary, Mother of God,
> pray for us sinners,
> now and at the hour of our death.
> Amen.

Bob went on with his story. "George recognized me in a newspaper article about former Roman Catholic priests who had married. He remembered that I am now the vicar of this Episcopal church and came to see me after he lost his job as a tutor and was about to be evicted from his apartment. I couldn't get over how old he looked—he had diabetes and was very sick." Bob put on a pot of coffee for the two of them, warmed up a meal for George from the parish kitchen's pantry, and pieced together enough money to pay his rent. He did not see George for several weeks—until George needed help again. Bob continued, "The second time he showed up, he was in terrible shape. His truck had fallen apart, and he had used his last dime for cab fare to the church. He broke down crying and told me he had decided to kill himself." Realizing how desperate the situation was, Bob came up with a quick excuse to slip out of the room, make a telephone call or two, and get George admitted into a treatment facility for stabilization.

Then came the hard part. George needed to go into assisted living for the three months before Medicaid and disability benefits would kick in, and Bob did not have that kind of money at his disposal. He prayed and fretted and prayed anew, until he realized he had to open the door he had carefully closed—presumably forever. Mustering his courage, he wrote to the head of the Franciscan Order—the community he chose to leave—and asked on George's behalf for "quite a bit of money." The plea went out into the far reaches of the Franciscan brotherhood, and very soon, Bob raised over five thousand dollars. But that was just the tip of the miracle. "The grace of God appeared to me in the form of letters and calls from people out of my past with whom I needed to be reconciled . . . significant people I've considered as good as dead . . . people for whom I was buried in a hole of broken promises . . . one priest I even hated!" Bob stopped short his story— "hate" is not a word that passes easily from his lips—and cast his gaze around an invisible circle of remembered faces. "It's as if this web of relationship had hung slack for too long a time, only waiting for a stir to rouse it back to life. The stir came from George."

About five months later, George's aunt called Bob. George was in the hospital in Atlanta with a ruptured colon, and the prognosis was bad. "I don't know why, but I resisted going to see him for a good while that day," Bob told me. "It was all I could do to put on my clerical shirt and walk into that room. Maybe I was afraid of seeing part of me lying there. I just don't know. . . .

"George was not able to respond—or at least not overtly—when I finally scraped up enough nerve to make my entrance. George's brother Paul was sitting by the bed, and the two of us swapped old stories for about forty-five minutes. Then, the machines went flat."

Bob took a moment before going on. "Paul at last nodded, and I read the prayer commending George into God's hands. It seems fitting that the ending speaks of an eternally expanding web— 'Receive him into the arms of your mercy . . . and into the glorious company of the saints in light.'"[5] Bob grinned and added, "I bet George's arrival once again caused quite a stir!"

Bob was planning the memorial service the day I drove down to see the new building into which the Church of the Nativity had now moved. He volunteered to conduct it, and Paul took him up on the offer. George's Roman Catholic family would all be there, and members of the Episcopal congregation would decorate the altar and serve lunch. I asked Bob what kind of service it would be. "Oh, I'll use appropriate readings from scripture and prayers, and I'll wear a suit—no vestments. I think that would be the best way to go. George would be comfortable with that." Bob gave me a broad smile. "His ashes will be the first ones placed in our memorial garden when it is completed in November. Paul will keep them until we're ready. And guess what else? In lieu of flowers, George's family asks that people make contributions to Nativity's building fund. Talk about a web of relationships!"

Spirals of connection now twirled and swirled inside me. The earthly remains of George—former Franciscan friar and now saint in light—will join those of hitherto unknown Episcopal sisters and brothers in the yet-unfinished garden of their church that is named for the holy birth. His ashes will be put in the ground by his Saint Joseph's classmate of long years ago—another onetime friar with whom he recited prayers through the Holy Mother. The two men found each other by virtue of the invisible bonds of their order—with perhaps some assistance from Mary herself. The old bluegrass hymn started rolling around in my head—"Will the circle be unbroken by and by, Lord, by and by? There's a better home awaiting in the sky, Lord, in the sky." Or maybe the better home is here right now—when webs get ruffled and loose strands are linked up in ways we could not possibly arrange on our own.

Bob had a few more things to say before I left him that day—stray musings directed more to himself than to me. "Strange—George's life went full circle. After all of his work with the homeless as a Franciscan, he himself became the indigent person Francis made a priority. People usually go around the other way." A pause. "And George never was an interpersonal kind of guy. He didn't know how to have a real relationship with anyone. Yet, ironically, it was through him and his willingness to come to me that so many of us got connected up again—and experienced healing. The saying may border on a churchy cliché, but God does work in mysterious ways."

Another pause. "Certain words of Francis have now taken on new meaning for this former friar: 'If a mother loves and cares for her child in the flesh, a friar should certainly love and care for his spiritual brother all the more tenderly.' Perhaps for a while, George carried them deeper in his heart than some of the rest of us did." Bob chuckled as if remembering a good joke. "I still can't get over the assisted living facility's name—'Dream Catcher Farm.' I wonder what kind of dreams people who live in such a place can have. Or maybe that's just the kind of place where eternal dreams take form. . . . I wonder about George's dreams." Bob shook his head. "He was an inconvenient intrusion at first. I'm now glad he came to my door. He made a difference."

From the Third Joy of the Franciscan Crown:

> Father, source of light in every age,
> the virgin conceived and bore your Son
>   who is called Wonderful God, Prince of Peace.
> May her prayer, the gift of a mother's love,
>   be your people's joy through all ages.

> May her response, born of a humble heart,
>   draw your Spirit to rest on your people.
> Grant this through Christ our Lord.
>   Amen.
> Mother of our Savior!
>   Pray for us.

Shortly after my conversation with Bob, I went to New York to visit my mother. I saw the trip—like George's showing up that morning—as an inconvenient intrusion into my busy summer. Mother lives in the town where I went to high school. She attends the small Presbyterian church where I was first confirmed and where I over again played the angel Gabriel in the Christmas pageant. I longed to be Mary, but tall for my age and loud of voice, I crawled up on the elders' bench year after year, struggling to balance the ungainly gilded cardboard wings, and repeated the inconceivable announcement of the Nativity—the improbable birth into our human family.

Mother and I drove around and looked at our old house and the site of my old school—believe it or not, now a facility for assisted living. I wonder if it is a place of dreams. As unbroken circles began to pick up steam and turn round and round, I felt the presence of my late father. The bond between us became almost tangible. Daddy rode the commuter train from this town into the city, religiously working the *New York Times* crossword puzzle along the way. I wonder if he was really all that predictable or if he ever dreamed wild dreams during those day-in and day-out journeys. Daddy was a brilliant man but, like George, not very good at relationships. I wonder what more could have been between us. I wonder what still might happen—as webs flutter and stir anew, as strands become reconnected in unexpected ways. I wonder if, like George, he could show up at the door.

He raises up the needy out of distress,
and makes their families like flocks.—Psalm 107

- What are my desires for community and my longings for relationship?
- What price will I pay if I come to live in the community of my desires?
- What graces will I need if I am to enter into the relationships for which I yearn?

God, you are three in one and one in three. Your nature is communal, and your will is for us to live in an ever-deepening and loving relationship with you and with each other. Grant that with your help, we may do everything in our power to restore the bonds of unity among us all in Christ. Amen.

———

Time Line   8

The days of our life are seventy years,
   or perhaps eighty, if we are strong;
even then their span is only toil and trouble;
   they are soon gone, and we fly away.—Psalm 90

VIRGINIA LOOKED IN THE MIRROR and saw what was for her
the face of a wrinkled old woman. My friend and I were
celebrating our seventieth and fiftieth birthdays just days apart,
and she said to me, "I wonder where that woman came from. I feel
no different inside from the girl I was at nineteen or twenty. . . ."
I was not quite far enough along at fifty to appreciate fully her
words. Then about ten years later, I attended a retreat and received the familiar instructions to represent my life journey in a
time-line format, indicating high and low points—periods when
I felt close to God and those when I had difficulty experiencing
God's presence at all. My effort looked rather like the graph trac-
ing a turbulent stock market—bull to bear and back again. But
what struck me did not, on the surface, have anything to do with
my relationship to God. Instead, the very length of the line itself
dismayed the young girl inside me. Six vertical marks divided it
into decades.

Lee is an Atlanta-based dancer and choreographer of some
renown, and we both attend Saint Luke's Episcopal Church. Every
Palm Sunday, I begin my Holy Week trek launched forth by the
liturgical dance she and members of her company offer: the joy-
ful and triumphant movements down the center aisle at the beginning of the service and Lee's solemn solo at the offertory, in

which images of the cross to come begin to emerge. She graciously agreed to talk to me about artistry and aging—even in the midst of her busy recital season. I figured it was within the bounds of tact to ask, since I was one mark ahead of her!

I arrived with two chicken sandwiches at the appointed hour. Lee, fresh from her studio with her black hair pulled severely back from her angular face, managed to look elegant in the likes of white sweat pants and a T-shirt. She directed me to the second-story, yellow-walled living room of her town house. I took out my notebook, and we two artists with our collective accumulation of eleven vertical strokes began.

"When did you start to dance?"

"I was five. I had flat feet and wore those wretched high-top shoes," Lee responded. "The podiatrist suggested that my parents enroll me in ballet classes." I silently wondered how often gifts are revealed through adversity or flaw. Lee then added a touch of nostalgia that only those of us with the requisite number of decade stripes can appreciate: "I remember looking at my feet inside the X-ray machine at Spainhour's Department Store." I peered back down the stretch of my own time line and saw the illuminated bones of my long, thin, and very flat feet.

Lee lived in the old family home—now the Catawba County Historical Association Museum—in Hickory, North Carolina. She studied with the Louis Nunnery School of Classical Ballet until she was seventeen, and every spring at the end of the recitals, Lee wept. "You see, we did not dance in the summer, and that was all I wanted to do." So she and her sister Dinny improvised, organizing their own classes of two—their *pas de deux*—until Lee was about thirteen and discovered a school in Asheville that taught off-season. The spring flood of tears was over and gone. "As often as I could, I took the two-hour train ride through the mountains, got off at the Biltmore stop, and walked to the studio." Later on, she studied at the summer honors program begun by then Governor Terry Sanford in Winston-Salem. She here met Richard England of the Juilliard School, who convinced her parents that it was time for her to head to New York.

Lee now dropped a poignant footnote into her story. "When our family recently sold our home to the county, we found an old tapestry in the attic." Lee proudly showed me the photograph of a lovely Renaissance maiden holding a lute. Referring to Isadora Duncan, the great innovator in interpretive dance, she exclaimed, "My muse, my Isadora, was there all along, keeping me company and steering me forward!" A bit wistfully she added, "I wish I had known."

Still shy of her second decade score, Lee auditioned and was accepted at both Juilliard and the New York School of American Ballet. Her father insisted that she go to the former because it offered a college degree. "I lasted only two years. I lived in the Barbizon and had no friends. It was a terrible time for a young girl from Hickory—or from anywhere else for that matter. I hated it!" Lee's salvation came when Governor Sanford established the North Carolina School of the Arts. There, she found her home and a proper mentor. The second mark finally appeared on her time line.

After graduation, Lee returned to New York for a period of about seven years—now to dance with Alvin Ailey and other prestigious companies as she continued her formation in the professional ranks. But the watershed call came in 1975, when she was teaching and dancing in Boone, North Carolina. Atlanta's eminent Robert Shaw, in conjunction with the Northside School of the Arts, invited her to choreograph Leonard Bernstein's *Mass*.

She had performed in the original production with Ailey at the Kennedy Center for the Performing Arts in Washington.

Even now, she voices her protest: "I never wanted to be a choreographer. I didn't think I had what it took—and besides, all I wanted to do was dance!"

Her father's influence weighed in again: "You can do it. You can learn how."

"And I did. That call changed my life. Having found that I do not have to perform in everything, I actually would rather choreograph." And choreograph she has—for the Atlanta Symphony, the Atlanta Opera, the Atlanta Contemporary Dance Company, and her own company—all the while, continuing the rigor of the dance, marrying, bearing two children, and gathering her remaining three vertical strokes.

"I dance everywhere I am—sometimes to the embarrassment of my family. I'm going to dance as long as I can." She shifted her long, lean body in her chair. "But the discipline is so hard. Even now, I take a lesson every day to keep myself in shape." A pause. "Being a good smiler has helped me out along the way. Smiling is better than crying." She then softly added, "I'm not sure I would choose the dancer's life if I had it to do over." I somehow did not believe her. As if reading my mind, she shifted her mood and broke into a wide grin. "These days, I prefer dancing solo—I get to call my own shots!"

The question I came to ask now formed on my lips: "When you can no longer dance, will you still be a dancer?" The question is key because, reworded, it is everyone else's as well: When I can no longer do—when the time-line strokes take their relentless toll—will I still be who I am? Lee's answer was reassuring in its swiftness. "Oh, I will always be a dancer. Dancing is the passion God places deep within me. It just will take different forms—like my painting. I dance on canvas—especially when we go to the beach. And I will paint even more later on."

I thought of another painter—Sara—whose hands are so crippled by rheumatoid arthritis that she can no longer hold a brush. She has not put oil to canvas in twenty years. I asked a relative of Sara's the same question: "Is she still a painter?"

His answer was as swift as Lee's. "Oh yes. She paints with her voice now. Sara is a poet, describing beauty and detail that without her help, I would never see."

Words of several artist friends emerged in my memory. Artists, perhaps, have to come to grips with the inevitability of change—inherent in the creative process—before the accumulating decade strokes thrust it upon the rest of us. Rob, an actor, sets the stage: "Creativity is what it means to be human. Everything we do is art, and everyone is storyteller, dancer, painter, singer, musician, actor. Each of us has it all—we're simply wired differently." And if his words are true, they raise the possibility that we can tap into these various parts of ourselves—what Lee calls "passions"—when the time is right, that we can move from dancer to painter to poet as the lines of our lives unfold.

Carolyn, a talented young Atlanta painter who incorporates an interesting collage technique into her works, contributes to Rob's conviction: "I say about a particular fragment that I am saving—an eye or a mouth, for example—'I just haven't used it yet. Its time will come.'" I think of the bits and pieces of stories waiting in my notebooks. I just have not used them yet. Their time has not yet come.

Taking this tack, we can consider every score along the time line as a theological event, an engagement with God. Each offers us a beribboned gift package to open—a present of surprise and possibility to unwrap and relish. Each also provides us with the opportunity to release what has been and to accept the person we both continue on to be and are becoming. I think this letting go and moving on is a definition of forgiveness—forgiving ourselves and God for what is happening to us and, at the same time, giving thanks for new opportunity to be ourselves. As my colleague O.K.—seven vertical stripes strong—regularly affirms, "Oh happy day!" And when he does, I see again the inscription on a plaque in a Canadian shop:

> Sing like there's nobody listening—
> Dance like there's nobody watching—
> Love like you'll never get hurt—
> Live like there's heaven on earth!

Lee—dancer, choreographer, painter—poet-to-be, perchance—was having thoughts of her own. We now picked up our conversation, and she talked about her long involvement in education, both in her studio and in local schools. "I don't really teach children and adults differently," she explained to me. "What I want to do is instill a sense of dignity and respect for self and for the other in every one of them—using the art of dance as my framework."

"Sounds like pretty basic baptismal covenant stuff," I commented.

"Faith and dance have always been interwoven in me. They are the warp and weft of my life's tapestry," Lee responded. "Don't forget: Dance is where the expression of religion began. I am a more religious person because of my dance, and I have become a better dancer because of my faith. The older I get, the more connected the two are for me."

Continuing, "I would never tell a child that she will not be a dancer—because who am I to say? I think 'making it' has less to do with talent than with those passions God places in us." Lee is preparing her students to open the bright gift packages they will receive along the length of their time lines—and in her teaching, she prepares herself as well.

> And I'll lead you all, wherever you may be,
> and I'll lead you all in the Dance, said he.[6]

> Singers and dancers alike say,
> > "All my springs are in you."—Psalm 87

- How does where I am on my time line enlighten who I am in my person?
- What price will I pay if I am to remain true to the one God intends me to be?
- What graces will I need if I am to journey faithfully on?

Dancer God, you leap both in and out of time. Bless us with an awareness of your presence in our lives, as together, we move to your song of love, meaning, and purpose. Amen.

The Center 9

 They walk around in darkness;
    all the foundations of the earth are shaken.—Psalm 82

TEN OF US SAT IN THE FRONT PEW of the dusky nave dressed in black, going forward to the lectern one by one to make our somber contributions to the service of Tenebrae: readings from the likes of the Lamentations of Jeremiah, interspersed with psalms sung by the choir. Tenebrae—Latin for "darkness" or "shadows"— is a Christian liturgy historically celebrated during the early days of Holy Week, and familiar as it has become over the years, its mounting drama always keeps me on edge.

After each reading, one of the candles in the triangular stand on the altar is extinguished, representing the desertion of Jesus by his disciples. With the tenth reading, the sole burning candle at the top—symbol of our Lord—is removed and hidden. The church becomes devoid of light, and, once again, we witness the forces of evil and death make their premature claim of victory—a claim I am each time afraid may hold.

The service then rolls on toward its solemn close and concluding collect, only to be stopped dead in its tracks by a shattering, "Not so fast!" A loud backstage crash simulates the resurrection's earthquake that splits history wide open: "This is not the end of the story. Actually, it has only begun." And even knowing in advance what is about to happen, I never fail to leap right out of my skin when that fearsome noise disrupts the sober progression of the liturgy. As my heart pounds away, the Christ candle is returned to the stand. By its light alone, we leave the church in silence, once again assured that the shadows will not prevail. We are now prepared to enter into the Triduum, those great three days that focus on Good Friday and end with the Vigil of Easter.

But on this night, the rude crash came too soon. I wondered if someone missed his cue. The choir had just finished singing the canticle, The Song of Zechariah—

> In the tender compassion of our God
>   the dawn from on high shall break upon us,
>   To shine on those who dwell in darkness and the
>   shadow of death,
>   and to guide our feet into the way of peace.

The congregation remained kneeling as an acolyte carried out that last lit candle, when—we later learned—a door banged open and shut, cutting through the hush of the dim nave. Three men— a stranger, a security guard, and one of our clergy—dashed down the center aisle. Their footsteps rang off the brick floor. Up to and past the freestanding altar they raced before exiting out a side aisle. They were in and gone before the congregation could do much more than blink. We are an in-town church, used to the wail of sirens and loud-spoken visitors popping in to protest one thing or another. But in the already unsettling context of Tenebrae, this mad charge was disconcerting.

Still, other than one or two parents who went to check on children in another part of the building, the rest of us remained immobile—for me, more in shock than in devotion. Fear of whatever else might be about to burst forth from the back of the room kept its fingers tight around the back of my neck. There was no way I could have turned my head to look around. For his part, the officiant never missed a beat, going right ahead with the anthem—"Christ for us became obedient unto death, even death on a cross. . . ." Then, as the choir began Allegri's haunting interpretation of Psalm 51, *Miserere mei, Deus*, he slipped out to see what was going on.

In retrospect, I decided that this particular musical accompaniment of the moment was perfect. Allegri's version has an exquisite soprano line that soars excruciatingly high over every third verse. The piece for me rolls pain and beauty into a cohesive whole, capturing the essence of the Good Friday-Easter event—and the heart of what it means to be human. This year, it served to set whatever pain lay behind that frantic chase into the solemn beauty of the Tenebrae liturgy: "Cast me not away from your presence and take not your holy Spirit from me." The death grip on my neck eased its hold.

The officiant returned to his station, and while he prayed the concluding collect, I, in turn, prayed that we would be spared the shattering noise that was yet to come. Enough was enough. But my prayer was not answered as I dictated—and appropriately so. CRASH! Of all years, this was the one in which we had to hear the earsplitting quake of victorious assurance. The acolyte brought the Christ candle back in, but this time we did not leave the church in shadowy silence. Instead, the overhead lights went on, and a lay leader instructed us to remain in our seats. He was a physician who had hurried back to check on the condition of the men, and he apprised us of the situation.

The pursuing priest and the security guard were able to apprehend the fleeing man and hold him until the police arrived. We learned that after being stopped for a traffic violation just a few blocks away, he shot an officer to death. Drugs likely were involved. Taking the policeman's vehicle, he soon abandoned it and took off on foot through the church's parking lot. He there attacked a late-arriving parishioner in an attempt to steal her car. She was shaken and bruised but not seriously hurt. Her screams alerted the security guard. The chase through the church ensued. The man was wounded in the leg in the fatal exchange of gunfire. His blood stained the carpet in the hallway beyond the nave.

After this update, the officiant offered prayers for the dead officer, his killer, and their families. And then we waited until the police completed their investigation. Heaven forbid: We were a crime scene in Holy Week! We made our way through a few hymns, but most of us did not feel like singing, so we softly talked among ourselves—or sat with our own unsettling thoughts. About an hour later, they released us into the cool and now darker-than-usual night.

Some long-forgotten words about violence and chaos made their way into my consciousness, and I searched for a poem I vaguely attributed to William Butler Yeats. I found it—"The Second Coming":

> Things fall apart; the centre cannot hold;
> Mere anarchy is loosed upon the world,
> The blood-dimmed tide is loosed, and everywhere
> The ceremony of innocence is drowned;
> The best lack all conviction, while the worst
> Are full of passionate intensity.[7]

Yeats wrote these words in 1919, in the context of the Russian Revolution and the rise of fascism in Europe. They seemed chillingly relevant to the events of the previous evening, portending that the "blood-dimmed tide" of brutality and aggression is simply a given of human existence.

The story of our excitement straightaway hit the local newspapers and television newscasts, and we firsthand observers had our fifteen minutes of fame, as neighbors and colleagues pressed us to tell what happened. I, for one, was initially delighted to oblige.

However, the novelty soon wore off, and disturbing realities and questions took its place. What indeed happened? First, the obvious: Unseemly violence broke into our service of worship, and one of our own was attacked on our grounds. "Things like this just do not happen in a church," we are prone to sputter—although the events of history vehemently disagree!

But the violent intrusion is finally not the real meat of the story. Its heart lies in the fact that the liturgy—the holy work of the people of God—went on. It and we did not fall apart. And we returned the following evening for the next occasion of Holy Week, Maundy Thursday—when we wash each other's feet and hear the great commandment to love and receive Jesus' promise of peace: "Peace is my last gift to you, my own peace I now leave with you; peace which the world cannot give, I give to you." I decided Yeats was wrong. The center—if it is the true center—holds. So maybe the church—where we find our central compass in God's peace—turns out to be the most fitting place of all to host invasion by the world's alarms.

Physicists now working in the field of chaos theory speak of the center. They say that beneath the randomness and chaos—the uncertainty—of our experience, there is a deep and abiding order. They call it the "strange attractor," which pulls everything to a core that holds. Albert Einstein is said to have asked, "Is the universe a friendly place?" All that he wrote and did indicates that his answer was yes: "I am satisfied with the mystery of the eternity of life and with the awareness and a glimpse of the marvelous structure of the existing world, together with the devoted striving to comprehend a portion, be it ever so tiny, of the Reason that manifests itself in nature."[8]

Considering God as the Strange Attractor catches my imagination. It speaks to my experience of a Holy Center who keeps pulling me in, who will not let me go—and which my limited faculties can only begin to embrace. Is the universe a friendly place? I think so—I hope so. After all, it is where I live, and I welcome the signs of an order in which I can place my trust.

In the fourth century, Saint Augustine wrote in *Confessions*, his unsurpassed spiritual autobiography: "Thou has made us for Thyself, and our heart is restless until it rests in Thee." No matter what distractions, confusions, and terrors confront us in this life, if we pay attention to the restlessness placed deep within us—in our centers—we can find ourselves marvelously drawn to the Center. We will never make sense of it all, but we can know the measure of resolution that makes it possible for us to move back and forth between day and night and day.

> For God alone my soul waits in silence;
>   from him comes my salvation.
> He alone is my rock and my salvation,
>   my fortress; I shall never be shaken.—Psalm 62

- How am I experiencing chaos, meaninglessness, or purposelessness in my life?
- What price will I pay if I allow God to place centeredness and peace amidst the chaos?
- What graces will I need if I am to accept the gift of God's self to sustain my life and my hope?

Ever-present God, for you alone our souls in silence wait. Bless us with an awareness of your presence in the manifold chances and changes of life, so that our hearts, set on you, may know its meaning and purpose and thus be not afraid. Amen.

———

The Incomplete Sentence 10

 The mighty one, God the Lord,
    speaks and summons the earth
    from the rising of the sun to its setting.—Psalm 50

THE EERIE BUGLING SOUND RANG through the forest's hush. I had never heard anything like it before and wondered if the music indeed came from some alien sphere. High above the Bow River in Banff National Park, my husband John and I sat down on the edge of the cliff, hoping it would ring out again. We were not disappointed. First came the high trumpeting song. Then, a huge bull elk, tossing his massive antlers, stepped out of trees just across the river from our perch. Wading into the shallow water, his voice a shofar, he called forth his herd of does. About twelve lovely females emerged to join him and cross over to a small, heavily wooded island where they would receive the seed of the next generation.

Hiking for a week in the Canadian Rockies, we made our way along the banks of rushing mountain streams and slipped and slid on treacherous glacial surfaces. We followed trails back into deep and silent forests, where I sensed invisible eyes tracking our every move. While evidence of unseen companions indeed abounded— bark freshly stripped off trees by the claws of bears and scat of various sizes along the tracks—the elk were the first we saw in the flesh. They gave us an answer to the question, who else is here?

Informational markers posted along our way helped, too. They did an exemplary job of telling about the very spots where we stood—both the contemporary story and the one depicting who and what had been there in ages past. We became caught up in the drama of the monumental geological events that had taken place hundreds of millions of years ago: mountains set on their sides, valleys lifted up, highways carved straight by the relentless fingers of icy sculptors. We stood in the fossil beds of great seas and touched stony evidence of teeming life long gone. And we could not help realizing that our own time was passing in the moment. The mountains soaring around us were even then being reshaped and torn down by rushing waters and grinding silt—perhaps best thought of as continuing contractions of divine labor. One day, they will be no more. Something else will stand in their stead.

Early on, I realized that I was pacing my stride to the tenor air from Handel's *Messiah*: "Every valley shall be exalted, and every mountain and hill made low. . . ." Over and over, I heard it in my inside ear and hummed along. The ensuing chorus soon clicked in as well: "And the glory of the Lord shall be revealed . . . for the mouth of the Lord hath spoken it."

Tennessee Williams provides a footnote to this Canadian adventure. Shortly after our return home, we went to see our friend Mary Lynn in Williams's play, *The Night of the Iguana*. I sat riveted to my seat, watching her become Hannah Jelkes, the impecunious and itinerant painter, who tenderly shepherds her grandfather Nonno, the aging poet, from stop to stop. The scene is the verandah of a sleazy Mexican hotel, and Shannon, the disgraced and neurotic priest, is recounting the circumstances leading to his first breakdown and departure from the church. His current line of work is leading tours: "Collecting evidence!"

"Evidence of what, Mr. Shannon?" Hannah asks.

He responds a touch shyly, "My personal idea of God, not as a senile delinquent, but as a . . ."

Hannah responds, "Incomplete sentence."[9]

The words "incomplete sentence" affected me like a brief jolt of electricity, and for an instant, I lost the story line of the play. I think Hannah is both noting that Shannon does not finish his thought and commenting on the nature of God, but the latter is what I heard: God—the Incomplete Sentence! I heard the stirring possibility that God is still working out the divine plan, that God is still making up the divine mind about what is yet to be—that maybe God has not quite decided what shape and form those Canadian mountains and valleys will take.

The thought that God has surprises in store for the divine self as well as for us excites and intrigues me—although I suspect that, at times, I will join Jonah and be infuriated with God for changing direction with the contemporary likes of Nineveh: "Compassion and relief are not what they deserve. Kill the bastards!" Nonetheless, the idea that history may take unexpected twists and turns ahead is the stuff of a good mystery book—with the plot unfolding even to the author as it moves along. While Good Friday-Easter gives us the story's ending—and I do not always resist the temptation to take a peek at the last page of my novel—we join God in not knowing how or when we will get there.

Make no mistake: The last sentence—the complete sentence—will be God's. I think this is part of what lies behind the commandment against crafting and worshiping idols and images. Not only can we look at these human-made artifacts as deities in their own right, but the very act of fashioning them also gives us the false belief that we can define who and what God is—that we can complete the sentence. Our icons and crucifixes and cathedrals—our sacred objects and places—are to be understood as artistic symbols, not ends to be revered on their own merit. For all their beauty and power, they, at best, only attempt to point beyond themselves toward the all-powerful God. We do well to remember that God's words to Moses—right at the beginning—were, "I am who I am. I will be what I will be." God might have added, "I am the one who will write the last words."

God writes that last sentence—places the final punctuation, an exclamation point—on Good Friday and Easter. God says in no uncertain terms, "It is finished: evil and death have no power! Creation is mine, and I will claim it and hold it close to my heart." To these ultimate words, God adds, "While the future is in my hands, I choose not to know how it will unfold along the way. I choose to be dependent—I would rather not labor alone. I prefer help with the composition." So God allows us—invites us—to participate in completing sentences. God renders the divine work vulnerable to our limited choice of words and our stilted phrasing. God seems to consider the price of mucked-up syntax, dead-end chapters, and awkward prayers worth our collaboration on the divine magnum opus. Reciprocal love is impossible when one side holds complete sway, and God is hoping that, together, we will compose a love story.

Mary Lynn, my actor friend, later reminded me that the notion of the incomplete sentence appears twice more in Williams's play, each time presenting Shannon or Hannah with the challenge to reveal something very personally honest—perhaps to share God. I like to think God, the Incomplete Sentence, yearns to be honest with us and wants us to be honest in return—so we can fall ever more deeply in love. But I also think God never intends us to know everything about the divine self, any more than I want my human lover to know everything about me—as if we could anyway. Such would spoil the mystery—and probably the loving. Ah, the incomplete sentence!

The Epiphany star is our sign. It shines with the opportunities God gives us to look for more and more God: "Lead us, who know you now by faith, to your presence, where we may see your glory face to face."[10] And God provides even more than the invitation of a bright star in the night sky. God pursues us in the course of our days through every means at hand—companions and strangers; events mundane and extraordinary; music that soars and thrills, music that soothes and lulls; the curving bodies of dancers; the curved bodies of those in rolling chairs; vivid paints on canvases; muted hues on the forest's floor. God is determined to write our story with us even when we run for all we are worth in the opposite direction. Francis Thompson, the English aesthetic poet of the 1890s, says it well in his most famous poem, "The Hound of Heaven":

> I fled Him, down the nights and down the days;
> I fled Him, down the arches of the years;
> I fled Him, down the labyrinthine ways
> Of my own mind; and in the midst of tears
> I hid from Him, and under running laughter.
>   Up vistaed hopes I sped;
>   And shot, precipitated,
> Adown Titanic glooms of chasméd fears,
>   From those strong feet that followed, followed after.
>   But with unhurrying chase,
>   And unperturbéd pace,
>   Deliberate speed, majestic instancy,
>   They beat—and a voice beat
>   More instant than the feet—
> "All things betray thee, who betrayest Me."[11]

I hear the divine panting. I feel God's hot breath upon my neck.

> Where can I go from your spirit?
> Or where can I flee from your presence?—Psalm 139

- What do I believe about God's presence and action in human life and history?
- What price will I pay if I acknowledge that God chooses to do nothing without our help?
- What graces will I need if I am to live a life of dependent cooperation with God?

Author God, write your word upon our hearts, that we may cooperate with you in completing the sentence—your dream for creation—which neither of us can bring to an end on our own. And all for your love's sake. Amen.

———

Praise the Lord with the lyre;
>   make melody to him with the harp of ten strings.
Sing to him a new song;
>   play skillfully on the strings, with loud shouts.—Psalm 33

E LIZABETH SLOWLY LOWERED HER BOW. Her left hand slid down the cello's neck into her lap, and she felt her whole body wrap limply around her instrument in exhaustion and exultation. The orchestra and chorus had come to the conclusion of Beethoven's Ninth Symphony, with its stirring fourth-movement setting of Friedrich Schiller's "Ode to Joy." The last triumphant notes echoed around the cavernous Schauspielhaus in East Berlin—as though they had taken on lives of their own but were reluctant to depart too quickly into the night of the world outside.

The audience went limp as well—rather like the response to a powerful orgasm—recognizing they had been part of an unrepeatable occasion. No one stirred for an eternity of seconds, and then, applause swelled and rose and rolled on and on. All came to their feet in a single, as-if-choreographed movement, and Maestro Shaw motioned the orchestra and chorus to rise with them. Every woman and man in the hall found themselves standing in each other's presence, basking in this all-too-brief celebration of their common humanity before God—in the city still so cruelly divided by hatred and fear. Schiller already described the moment: *Alle Menschen werden Brüder*—"All men become brothers under the sway of thy gentle wings."

The date was May 1988—a year and a half before the wall would be punched open and Berliners could travel freely back and forth for the first time since August 1961. Elizabeth and her violist husband Paul were on a European tour with Robert Shaw and over 340 members of the Atlanta Symphony and Chorus. They described this particular performance to me as "one of those miraculous, spontaneous occasions when everything comes together as never before and you know you have participated in an event exceeding your efforts and your expectations—an event beyond yourselves."

"You can't force it," Elizabeth added when they attempted to recount the evening to me. "It just happens, and you never know when. That's the mystery."

Paul did his best to offer an explanation, "Everyone's senses are pointed in the same direction and . . ." He stopped, embarrassed, realizing that he was coming up short. I, in turn, could only intuit what had taken place by the rapt expressions on their faces as they traveled back over the years to East Berlin. Paul broke our reverie, "I wonder if we somehow were aware of a new spirit let loose in the air that night—a spirit that passed through us into the audience and out into the streets."

They then shifted to another time when everything once again came together. It was the spring of 1989, and they were in Avery Fisher Hall on the other side of the podium. Leonard Bernstein conducted the New York Philharmonic Orchestra in Gustav Mahler's Second Symphony, *Resurrection*. Friedrich Klopstock's Resurrection hymn, "Auferstehung," provides words for the fifth movement's breathtaking choral finale—to which Mahler contributes his own:

> Arise, yes, you will arise,
> Dust of my body, after a brief rest!
> Immortal life
> Will he, who called you, grant to you.
>
> You are sown that you might bloom again!
> The Lord of harvest goes
> And gathers sheaves,
> Gathers us, who died.

Oh, believe, my heart, nothing is lost for you!
Yours, yes, yours alone is what you longed for,
What you loved, and what you fought for.

Oh believe, you were not born in vain,
That which was created must perish,
What perished will arise!
No longer tremble!
Prepare to live!

Oh agony, you piercing pain,
From you I have escaped!
Oh death, all-conquering claim
Now you are defeated!

With wings that I have gained,
In seeking to perfect my love
Will I ascend
Into the light which no eye has ever reached.

With wings that I have gained
Will I ascend.
I will die to be alive!

Arise, you will arise,
My heart, within a moment!
What you have conquered,
To God, to God it will bear you up.[12]

Elizabeth and Paul left the hall numb, yet with every nerve ending in their bodies starkly alert. The last notes—heaven gloriously heard—still crashed around them as they walked back to their hotel in tears. Oh, believe, my heart, believe! My response to

Mahler is, "Oh yes, I believe! How could I not? You escort me to the very gates of paradise!" I have never made it through that last movement with dry eyes.

Robert Shaw spoke of art as "Flesh become Word," prompting me to consider all who contribute to this "true transubstantiation." First, there is the artist—in this case the composer of the symphony, who first hears the music and commits it to his manuscript, careful to listen for the voices of the various instruments as they speak to and around one another. In one sense, the piece is finished when he makes his last notation—or the painter brushes the final stroke on her canvas. But in another, the work is not complete until someone decides to interpret and play it—or hang it on a wall where it can be viewed and appreciated—or even misinterpreted.

The orchestra might say that the work is consummated on the stage. Paul, now the associate principal violist with the Atlanta Symphony, describes playing in an orchestra as "being part of an ocean of sound, a living piece of art that rolls inexorably along." He continues, "Each musician must stay true to his own voice and still be part of that organic whole. The best conductors are attuned to this delicate and necessary tension." The paradox: Release of individualistic freedom while contributing one's personal power to the communal effort allows for the free flow of artistic expression. This is the fundamental paradox and truth of any community: Real freedom must always be in the service of something outside itself, or the result is the distortion of self-absorbed sin.

And then, there is the audience—or the patrons of the art museum. Someone has named the space between the orchestra and the audience the "mystic gulf"—where the alchemy happens. Shaw might have described it as the place where the bread and wine of the music become the body and blood of God. Wise conductors do not violate that crucible too often. They choose not to come out and explain the concert before it comes to pass. They know that they have no idea how it will finally come to pass—before the audience takes up its own instruments of hearing and interpretation and accompanies the orchestra's best efforts of the moment.

The naming of the sacred mystic gulf helps me understand why I have so much difficulty with a spate of announcements—untimely explanations—intruding on a congregation's course of worship, interrupting movement from word to table, throwing them off track. It helps me understand why I prefer the designation "president" to "celebrant." Heads of table are to preside for the people, not consider themselves responsible for performing ecclesial magic. And members of the congregation are active participants in the business at hand, playing their essential parts—seeing, hearing, praying, preparing to move forth. After all, liturgy is defined as the work of the people. I think it is sweaty, demanding work—not idle amusement for passive occupants of pews.

Both the concert hall and the worship space are places where the sacramental dimensions of life are to hold sway—where we become aware of what otherwise would be hidden. Their offerings can be consummated in uncounted ways even after the performance or the service is over, as fingers continue to fly over unseen strings, as vibratos still tremble in hearts and heads, as the prayers of the people rise with the altar's incense—as transubstantiation, flesh becoming Word, is realized. The souls who make music together will be touched and lifted—even to the gates of heaven. Ascending, smoky prayers will take on lives of their own as they carry transforming power into the world beyond—where cruel walls can come tumbling down.

> Praise him with trumpet sound;
>   praise him with lute and harp!
> Praise him with tambourine and dance;

> praise him with strings and pipe!
> Praise him with clanging cymbals;
> praise him with loud clashing cymbals!
> Let everything that breathes praise the Lord!
> Praise the Lord!—Psalm 150

- How do I experience the sacred, mystic gulfs of life?
- What price will I pay if am to respect and not violate them?
- What graces will I need if I am to allow for occasions of transubstantiation?

Mysterious, immanent God, help us who are flesh participate in the coming of your living Word. And all for your glory and praise. Amen.

———

Vessels 12

Hear my prayer, O Lord,
   and give ear to my cry;
   do not hold your peace at my tears.—Psalm 39

THE STOUT, GRAY-HAIRED WOMAN and a younger man, both dressed in black, slipped quietly into Giana's Soho pottery shop one afternoon and began looking around. The woman finally selected a large lidded pot and, in broken English, inquired as to the price. When Giana answered, the woman's eyes flooded with pain. "Have I marked it too high?" Giana anxiously asked. "I'm sure we can work something out."

The man then spoke. His English was barely better. "The price is fine. We are seeking an urn to hold my father's ashes. My mother's grief sometimes is too much for her."

"I don't know where the idea came from," Giana later told me, "but I heard myself suggesting that together—now—we make the vessel she needed." The woman understood, nodded her agreement, and stood next to Giana at the wheel, hands clasped together in front of her. Her son took his place behind them, arms nervously folded across his chest.

Giana continued, "She watched the clay as I kneaded, centered, and started pulling it upward from the wheel. Soon, her hands came up and began forming the shape she wanted the urn to take. 'A little higher,' she gestured, 'and a little fuller.' I watched and followed her lead." The woman began to relax. The son breathed out audibly in relief; his arms dropped. Giana completed the throwing, and they talked about the glazes she would use.

When the woman returned a few days later for the finished urn, she was able to manage a faint smile. "Thank you for helping," she said.

"But I just made a pot," Giana responded; "it's what I do." "Nothing special," she thought to herself. She was wrong. The urn was a first—not to be the last.

Giana—named for the composer of operas, Gian Carlo Menotti —was in her twenties during those Soho years. She had completed a rigorous apprenticeship in Japan, and, on the surface, she had it all—accounts with Macy's, Bergdorf Goodman, Tiffany, Gucci; reviews in the *New York Times*. Her pottery and the gallery were in a Columbia Pictures movie set; *House Beautiful* featured her work. Still, an element was missing for her even in the midst of all that success. "As an artist, you feel you should have something to say," she confessed, "and I knew I had no statement to make. I felt fragmented and scattered; I wasn't very deep. I did everything from the gut—a childish approach, I thought."

Then at twenty-six, her lot changed with a diagnosis of Hodgkin's disease. Giana lost the gallery and all her trappings. "I went home to Long Island," she said, "with only a suitcase in hand to live with my mother while I completed my treatments. After that, I zigzagged around the country with my suitcase—to Arizona, Colorado, and Florida; back to New York and on to California. I don't know what I was looking for. Mostly, I was grieving—for myself and all I had lost." She added softly—more to herself than to me—"How debilitating unresolved grief can be."

Giana finally drove into Florence, Oregon, at six o'clock on a dismal and dank morning. She liked the looks of the shops and galleries and restaurants she passed. It seemed like a place where she could live and work. However, nothing was open so she proceeded on outside the town to an ocean overlook and parked.

"I am not a religious person," Giana made plain, "not since I was a child and I ran away to the convent. I experienced their telling me lies. Later, I felt alone and abandoned during my illness. I do not pray."

But then she went on, "That early morning, I did: 'God, I am tired. I'm ready for things to come together. This town seems perfect. I need a sign.'" The clouds opened, and rays of sunlight sparkled onto the water below. Giana murmured out loud, "Thank you," and drove back into Florence. She met and married John Eden in Oregon, and they had their first child, Luke. The family soon moved back to John's hometown of Jesup, deep in southern Georgia, where a daughter, Liana, was born.

Both babies' deliveries were difficult. While still in the hospital the second time, Giana received two devastating blows: Her best friend from childhood, Michael, and her Uncle Rocco died of AIDS. Michael's death came almost at the moment of her daughter's birth; Rocco's, a few days later.

"I lost contact with Michael over the years," she told me. "He was not able to handle my illness very well. Rocco and I had had a special relationship during my New York days. He helped me set up the Soho gallery. We often ate dinner together and went out dancing. But he was living in Europe when I became sick, so he wasn't around either." Silence. "And I wasn't present for them. Now, I was in bed and couldn't even go to their funerals." Waves of grief and guilt continued to wash over Giana as the weeks went by, and her sense of urgency grew. She had to do something!

"At first, I considered making puppets," she allowed, "but that didn't seem quite right. So I turned to my potter's wheel and began two pieces simultaneously—one for Rocco and the other for Michael. I covered them with images and symbols that spoke of their spirits and their lives—glasses of wine, Kent cigarettes, musical notes, a poem, the Long Island shore where we grew up."

Giana was quick to add, "I did it for me. Through the urns, I could hold onto something of them. I could make up for some of the loss and hurt. Their creation brought real comfort to me, and I began to heal."

Giana took a job with a Jesup doctor who treats patients with AIDS. "Early on," she recounted, "I met Bill. His partner had recently died. What began as a trickle of words became a flood, as he poured out his love and his sorrow. I took his sadness inside me in the three hours I spent with him. Images swirled in my head, and I had what I call a 'vision.' Not the weird kind," she reassured me, humming a bar from a horror film sound track. "What I mean is that a picture formed. I drew a sketch and knew I had to make the piece for him. I built it up in the form of bricks, representing the strength of the relationship. I incorporated a black-and-white encircling band—a swirl—representing difficulties they had faced together. I attached the leaves to the swirl that his partner loved to rake. I mischievously included a marijuana leaf and placed a key ring on top of the lid. Keys were a big deal to him." The urn had power that visibly moved and comforted Bill when Giana presented it to him.

With the encouragement of the doctor and other members of the AIDS community, Giana set up her studio in Jesup, where she makes handsome dinnerware and goblets and bowls—as well as the funerary urns. Most of her regular business is wholesale through stores and shops around the country. On the other hand, her efforts with the dying and their loved ones is very personal and consuming—one-on-one. I read an article about her in the *Atlanta Journal-Constitution* and drove the two hundred fifty miles to Jesup to hear her story firsthand.

"I follow the same process I did instinctively with Bill," she explained. "I interview and listen and learn about the essence of the dying or dead person's life—likes and dislikes, special interests and habits. I take in as much of the grief and pain as I can. People are very different in the ability to express their sadness. Then, the vision comes, and I make a sketch. If my concept meets with approval, I throw the urn, pouring all that I am carrying inside me into its creation. It is very difficult work." Giana becomes the vessel to hold another's grief. She decants it into the vessel she creates, and pain is transformed into beauty. "I want to give these families something back, something tangible they can hold and touch," she said. The word "compassion" comes to mind. It derives from the Latin *compati*—to suffer together.

"Are you ever afraid you will not be able to empty yourself— that you will just store up layer upon layer of sorrow?" I asked.

"No," she answered. "I always make two urns. The extra is for me. I keep little pieces of those I have come to know so well—and through them, experience healing myself. None are for sale." Giana took me out to her studio behind the family home on Hickory Street, and I saw the shelf of vessels—including those for Michael and Rocco and even ones for a cat and a dog. She has made about twenty in all, conducting some of her interviews over long distance. "I never know how much to charge," she confessed. "I accept whatever people send. Usually, it is more than enough."

Now in her forties, Giana has found her artistic voice. She writes, "As an artist, these urns are for me the ultimate gift that I can give . . . a tribute to the passing lives of those who are loved." With every one she throws, she makes the powerful statement that death never has the last word. She affirms that hurt and loss can be transformed into beauty and blessing. But Giana still insists she is not a religious person: "I don't have the relationship with God that other people do. I felt like a hypocrite the times I tried to go to church." I waited, sensing she had more to say. "My spirituality is in my work. My religion is in my work. Making these urns and helping these people is my tithe." She smiled a little self-consciously at her choice of words and continued, "The Japanese teach that it is not important to be famous—a big name. What's important is what you do. I am happy being in this little town, in this little shop. I am amazed that the grief work is what is reaching out. It is much more satisfying than anything I did in New York. And I'm the one who actually receives the gift: my own grounding."

I had many hours to reflect on the day during the drive back to Atlanta—a beautiful bowl with an intricate quilted design safely packed on the back seat. Along the way, I remembered Frederick Buechner's definition of vocation:

> It comes from the Latin *vocare*, to call, and means the work a man [sic] is called to by God. . . . The kind of work God usually calls you to is the kind of work (a) that you need most to do and (b) that the world most needs to have done. . . . Neither the hair shirt not the soft berth will do. The place God calls you to is the place where your deep gladness and the world's deep hunger meet.[13]

The God talk is Buechner's and mine—not Giana's. I will not be disrespectful and ascribe it to her. I am not sure God always cares about the names and labels we give to things anyway. That said, I am struck with how her labors fill the bill: her deep gladness straight on meeting the world's deep hunger. For me—and I believe, for the God I try to serve—she is engaged in holy work. I stand in awe of the courage required on her part voluntarily to take in all that pain and somehow do something lovely with it. Vessel creates healing vessel.

Then, on the outskirts of Atlanta, the familiar prayer attributed to Saint Francis moved into my consciousness. I changed two words:

Lord, make us vessels of your peace. Where there is hatred, let us pour love; where there is injury, pardon; where there is discord, union; where there is doubt, faith; where there is despair, hope; where there is darkness, light; where there is sadness, joy. Grant that we may not so much seek to be consoled as to console; to be understood as to understand; to be loved as to love. For it is in giving that we receive; it is in pardoning that we are pardoned; and it is in dying that we are born to eternal life.

When I presented the quilted bowl to my husband John, he saw a pattern of crosses that I had missed—and Giana had never intended as religious symbols. Those crosses led me to think of God as vessel—accepting and containing all the pain and sin the world could pour in, so they could be stirred up and made into life. My thoughts went on to the young girl Mary, the one asked to carry the divine seed—to be the *Theotokos*, the God bearer. She said yes; she consented—while heaven held its collective breath in anticipation. Vessel would give birth to transforming vessel.

> But you do see! Indeed you note trouble and grief,
> that you may take it into your hands.—Psalm 10

- How might I be a healing presence in the lives of others?
- What price will I pay if I am to devote myself to this work?
- What graces will I need if I am to find the courage to do so?

Comforting God, help us know the transforming power of your love, and by the might of your Holy Spirit, empower us to be holy vessels overflowing with your peace. Amen.

———

I have been entrusted to you ever since I was born;
you were my God when I was still in my mother's womb.
—Psalm 22 (BCP)

WHEN THE WINTER SNOWS melted and the spring rains came, the Susquehanna River ran fierce and high, leaving its bounds and pouring treacherous waters into our neighborhood in Endicott, New York. We moved to 608 South Liberty Avenue when I was in the fourth grade, and only another modest residence and a narrow street separated us from the river, even in its serene moments. This proximity kept my mother in a state of fear for the lives of her children, particularly that of my younger brother Benjamin. A toddler drowned a few years before our coming, so the Susquehanna meant death to her. It was her sworn enemy.

But the river was my friend. The same waters that flooded the street and left deposits of grass-killing silt carved out marvelous underground chambers back among the roots of the old sentinel trees guarding its banks. My mother had no idea how often I went to those caves, sliding down the smooth-polished bank and crawling into a beckoning opening on hands and knees—purposefully heading where I was not supposed to go. True, both the thrill of rebellion and the promise of sanctuary drew me there, but I also just delighted in the mud and the muck. This was my season of blue jeans and pocketknives in lieu of dresses and lipstick.

Some of the caves were single dens; others offered multiple nooks and crannies connected by narrow passageways. None was very large, so I had to assume a sitting-up, fetal position, and the posture was apt. My visits to these earthy wombs were periods of formation for me. My imagination took wing and soared as I dreamed about what I would do with my life. I remember wondering about the existence of God, even as I constructed determined and deliberate prayers. I took a small Bible on occasion, bent on reading through the Gospels. It seemed like a good thing to do at the time. I do not remember completing the task.

Death was in the mix too—I could smell it. The floodwaters that carved out delivery rooms for the young girl deposited rotting life-forms in their wake. Birth and death indeed joined together among the roots of the old trees, and a spasm of foreboding coupled with my excitement and expectation as I began each creeping entrance—all the while praying that I would not encounter one of the scavenging rats that came to the underground river world to dine. These were the days I began contemplating my own dying, but it was only a far-off thing then, difficult to imagine.

The allure of the cave caught up with me once more while on a trip to the Holy Land, where underground waters work away at the soluble limestone layers, forming W. H. Auden's "secret system of caves and conduits"[14]—dwellings, hiding places, tombs, places of birth. Early tradition has it that Jesus was born in a cave close to the village of Bethlehem, the inn of our familiar account, an extended grotto. I like to imagine that in a gesture of compassion to the young woman so heavy with child—in contrast to the harsh, "We have no room!"—the keeper took the couple around to the stone chamber where he boarded the animals, providing for them a modicum of privacy. I also like the idea of God's emerging from the protecting womb of his mortal mother into a womblike, cavernous shelter—"What could be more like Mother or a fitter background for her son? . . . "[15] It is as if the Eternal Mystery took cloistered time to pause and adapt to the thin air of earth before venturing forth.

I approached the birthing caves of Bethlehem with a mix of thrill and fear, much as I did those river caves years ago. But perhaps this is the only way one should draw near the spot where his first wails rang off ceiling and sides of limestone rock. The caves lie underneath the basilica of the Church of the Nativity, and I descended a curving, stone staircase to reach them. Joining hands with the long stream of pilgrims who have made their own silent passage down, I reached out and steadied myself against the cold, smooth wall. The main room was darkly afire with smoky lamps and candles, and I lit a narrow taper before taking my turn to kneel and crawl into the small opening marking the site of his birth. Inside is a fourteen-point silver star with the Latin inscription: HIC DE MARIA VIRGINE JESUS CHRISTUS NATUS EST. I rubbed its surface, brightly polished by the oil of so many beholden fingertips, and then touched its cool face with my lips.

The Cave of the Manger is down there too, the place of the three kings' visit of homage to the baby. As I climbed back up a second curve of stone stairs to the basilica and the street, I recalled T. S. Eliot's disquieting lines regarding their departure:

> . . . were we led all that way for
> Birth or Death? There was a Birth, certainly,
> We had evidence and no doubt. I had seen birth and death,
> But had thought they were different; this Birth was
> Hard and bitter agony for us, like Death, our death.
> We returned to our places, these Kingdoms,
> But no longer at ease here, in the old dispensation,
> With an alien people clutching their gods.
> I should be glad of another death.[16]

For a time, I wished the poet's words had not rattled my reveries. But of course, they must if the Birth is to be anything more than a sentimental social-call—a divine dropping by to say hello and see how things are going. Without the Death, the Birth would have made no difference. Without the Death, we would be forever stuck in our old dispensations, the alien kingdoms where we fret and fuss—grim and final death our sole and sad reprieve. The real birthing caves are the caves of the Holy Sepulchre, hewn out of the very bedrock of Golgotha—caves one approaches with trembling knees and hands covering eyes, praying he is not still there after all. Ever so slowly, I reached out to touch that looming rock, as though it were stone white-hot enough to sear my flesh. This was no place for gentle kisses. I wondered if those well-traveled magi ever made it back again—to the caves of his dying.

Upon my return home from the Holy Land, I came across an arresting set of hand-painted resin figures entitled "Affirmation of Faith." The central piece is an arched cave. The open carved-out side provides shelter for the holy family. Mary sleeps on a straw mat while Joseph, sitting with one leg bent and tucked under the other, gazes down at the baby he holds on his knee. Two brown-faced sheep complete this part of the collection. On the convex side, the artist painted a door. The other half of the figures includes a white-robed young man perched atop a large round stone, hair blowing behind him, and two startled women, staring at the scene with disbelieving faces. Right here is the whole story. He was born among us in a cave. He died and was buried in a cave-like tomb, hewn out of an abandoned limestone quarry on the outskirts of Jerusalem—literally, "the stone that the builders rejected." And neither cave could finally hold him.

> . . . but when I try to imagine a faultless love
>   Or the life to come, what I hear is the murmur
> Of underground streams, what I see is a limestone
>   landscape.[17]

The murmuring underground streams are the waters of baptism. They carve out the landscape and render it green. They do not allow us to linger too long in the caves of our childhood or in the grottos of Bethlehem. They carry us on to the royal limestone of Jerusalem—to the rock of Golgotha and the empty cave of the tomb. They are the waters in which we drown so we can be born. They are the cool waters we drink on the fourth day.

> He made streams come out of the rock,
>   and caused waters to flow down like rivers.—Psalm 78

- What in my life needs to die so something else can be born?
- What price will I pay if I receive this gift of new life?
- What graces will I need if I am to trust in God's transforming love?

Almighty, redeeming God, you demonstrated in Jesus your ability to bring life out of death. Help us to know that only in our willingness to die can we hope in new life through the power of your Holy Spirit. Amen.

Outstretched Arms 14

I stretch out my hands to you;
　　my soul thirsts for you like a parched land.—Psalm 143

T HE TAXI CARRYING MY HUSBAND John and me to our hotel
swept along Beach Avenue in the English Bay section of
Vancouver. A waterfront park bounded the bay to our left. You
could sense the water more than see it. The late afternoon was
drizzly and foggy, and the closed windows of the car muted sur-
rounding sounds. A few resolute walkers moved along the sidewalk,
covered heads bowed and hands stuffed deep down into raincoat
pockets. Suddenly, out of nowhere, a looming presence wrapped
in wispy shrouds of fog appeared in the park. Just as quickly, the
weather closed back in, and I lost sight of it.

"What was that?" I asked the driver. He shrugged, "Beats me. I
haven't lived here long. I guess it's some kind of monument." I
squinted and peered out again, this time catching a glimpse of what
appeared to be a human form. Or was it a cross? I turned around in
the cab for a further look through the back window, but then the
fog closed in for good. At that moment, we pulled up to our destination, and any thought of my mysterious sighting evaporated into
the hustle of checking in and finding our room.

By the next morning, the sky was bright and clear, and a brisk
breeze raised dancing whitecaps on the bay's face. Bikers, in-
line skaters, and parents pushing strollers swelled the number of
walkers and joggers, as the entire city poured out into the streets
and turned its collective face toward the sun. John and I were
right there with them. We wasted no time crossing the street

and covering the short distance down the park's walkway to . . . whatever it was.

The bronze plaque gave me its name: Inukshuk, meaning "likeness of man" in the language of the Inuit people, keepers of the ancient culture of the northern lands. Commissioned for the city of Vancouver by the government of the Northwest Territories, this Inukshuk towers above the combined height of three men. Six blocks of carved gray granite, perfectly balanced with each other, rise off a massive base. The first two stand vertically with a space in between—the legs. The next rests horizontally on them—the pelvis and waist. The fourth is a vertical member—the torso. The fifth is a horizontal block suggesting arms. The sixth rises vertically as the neck and head. Here indeed was the glimpse of humanity I caught through the fog. And it did not take too much imagination to see the top three pieces—vertical, horizontal, vertical—as a chunky cruciform image. Without thinking, I signed myself with the cross, and then looked around, a little self-consciously, to see if anyone noticed.

As we walked farther on along the bay, we came upon a colony of much smaller Inukshuit, built on logs and rocks at the water's edge. Some had longer arms; others, heftier legs. They were a tall and short, wide and thin population—just like those of us delighting in them and just like those who put them in place. I later learned that Inukshuit are familiar symbols of hospitality in Northern Canada, traditionally used by the Inuit people as landmark and navigational aids in the treeless tundra. When two tribes split, they may leave behind an Inukshuk to mark their next meeting place. Piles of rock show where fish, caribou, or a safe channel for passage can be found. Their builders adhere to a rule of generosity and friendship in a land that can be cold and barren.

There was no doubt about it. The Inukshuit had me in their thrall. I checked them out on roadsides and in galleries, and I finally bought a small serpentine carving by a young Cape Dorset sculptor to take home. Thirteen perfectly balanced green stones rise in human likeness off their base. The horizontal member is the most dramatic: Representing arms, it is as long as the rest of the piece is high. Inukshuk . . . likeness of man . . . with arms outstretched wide! Paul's words to the Philippians blaze across my consciousness: "And being found in human form, he humbled himself and became obedient to the point of death—even death on a cross." The words from the first story of my shared tradition soon follow: "So God created humankind in his image, in the image of God he created them; male and female he created them."

As far back as I can remember, I matter-of-factly accepted these early lines of Genesis—and relished them. "God's image? Of course, why not?" the self-centered child allowed. Over the years, my identification as God's offspring provided me with a sense of well-being and worth—especially welcome when I was hard-pressed to find it anywhere else. But in fits and starts, I have come to realize the complexities of the picture—or perhaps better said, its profound simplicities.

First of all, I am not the only one. The family is large, and it can be contentious. I have to elbow my way around if I am going to hold onto my rightful place at the center of things. And as elbows fly, defending what I deserve—my licit claim—can become dangerous and consuming. Words like "respect the dignity of every human being" lose their punch in the heat of the tribal battle. It is every divine image for herself. Outstretched arms would be foolish. Arms that are outstretched cannot punch and flail, cannot hold weapons, and there are not enough caribou and fish to go around in this cold and barren land. I have to do what I have to do to protect my own good and that of my limited circle of loved ones. Simple as that.

And also for as long as I can remember, I have struggled to come to grips with the staggering claim that once upon a time, God took human form and moved into the midst of our contention and chaos. Some days, the picture is quite clear. I see Jesus out there walking around, healing and teaching, dying and bursting out of the tomb, and I say, "Yes, of course—God-with-Us. Why not?" On those days, it makes perfect sense that God would step into God's own likeness to see if showing up could help us get it right—this business of being in the image of God.

And then at other times, when I stand in the face of the Great Mystery, the picture gets blurred and hazy. Even shaking my head to clear my vision doesn't bring it into focus. The question becomes "why?" Why would setting things straight make that much difference to God? Why wouldn't God just scratch us off as an experiment gone awry and try again somewhere else? It has to be more than divine pride. After all, becoming one of us results in those awful outstretched arms on a cross and a great deal of pain. God knows from the beginning how it will turn out in the end, so why not avoid that miserable scenario altogether and save the divine self a great deal of trouble?

The only answer I have been able to come up with is that it is a matter of character. Simple as that. If God had washed the divine hands of the whole mess, God would not be the god who God says God is. God would be a god who takes the easy way out, who does not care a whole lot about much of anything. God would be a god who dodges cost and pain, and being in that likeness would mean that we could shun them too. Stretching out our arms, pointing to safe passage and home—building an Inukshuk or taking up a cross—would be a foolish undertaking. We would be better served by pulling in our arms, wrapping them tightly around ourselves, and turning the other way—hiding our private parts of vulnerability. Hoarding caribou would indeed be the only sensible course of action. But the price? It would be the forfeiture of our humanity—if we truly believe we are created in the image of the God who does not dodge. So it then becomes a matter of character for us as well. Simple as that.

All said, the bequest of the hospitable Inukshuit of the northern lands still goes beyond their taking me on a trip into my own faith heritage—even one of deepened understanding. They raise for me a startling possibility: that of a universal cruciform symbol for the divine coupling with humanity. They expand Jesus' words about being the way, the truth, and the life and no one coming to God except through him far beyond any narrowly arrogant Christian interpretation. They link me up with past and future generations of peoples who do not speak of God in my familiar terms, who do not know Jesus as I claim and hope to know him, whose sacred stories are not the same as mine, but who nonetheless know the posture of the outstretched arms—the posture of hospitality and deliverance.

I suppose those who make it their business to study such things could shed light on my wonderings. However, for now, I do not want their insight. It would make no difference to me. For now, I delight in imagining a string of cross-shaped Inukshuit—by whatever names they are called—arms interlocked, twined around the globe, even lacing together the expanses of space—a vanguard against the Evil One.

> With a strong hand and an outstretched arm,
> for his steadfast love endures forever.—Psalm 136

- What have I seen that might point anew to God were I open to the possibility?
- What price will I pay if I acknowledge these fresh revelations of God's nature?
- What graces will I need if I am to receive further insights into God's character?

Ever-faithful God, you are continuously striving to reveal to us different ways of knowing who you are and how you act. Enable us to be alert to your disclosures and accepting of what we have difficulty understanding. Amen.

―――――

To allow mystery, which is to say to yourself, "There could be more, there could be things we don't understand," is not to damn knowledge. It is to take a wider view.

—Barry Holstun Lopez, *Of Wolves and Men*

Notes

1. Albert Einstein, "The World As I See It," *Ideas and Opinions* (New York: The Modern Library, 1994), 11–12.

2. From the commemorative program honoring Robert Shaw, a companion piece to the Atlanta Symphony Orchestra's performances of Haydn's *Seasons*, March 25–27, 1999.

3. James Weldon Johnson, "The Creation: A Negro Sermon," *Chapters into Verse: Poetry in English Inspired by the Bible*, vol. 1, ed. Robert Atwan and Laurance Wieder (New York: Oxford University Press, 1993), 21. Used by permission.

4. W. H. Auden, chorus from "For the Time Being, a Christmas Oratorio," *Collected Poems/W. H. Auden*, ed. Edward Mendelson (New York: Vintage International, 1991), 400. Used by permission.

5. Episcopal Church, *The Book of Common Prayer* (New York: Church Hymnal Corp., 1979), 465. Used by permission.

6. From Sydney Carter, *Lord of the Dance* (London: Stainer and Bell, 1963). Used by permission.

7. William Butler Yeats, "The Second Coming," *Chapters into Verse*, vol. 2, 376. Used by permission of Scribner, a Division of Simon & Schuster.

8. Einstein, "The World As I See It," 12.

9. Tennessee Williams, *The Night of the Iguana*, *Three by Tennessee:* Sweet Bird of Youth; The Rose Tattoo; The Night of the Iguana (New York: Modern American Library, 1976), 60–61. Used by permission.

10. Episcopal Church, *The Book of Common Prayer*, 214. Used by permission.

11. Francis Thompson, "The Hound of Heaven," *Chapters into Verse* vol. 2, 186–87.

12. Constantin Floros, *Gustav Mahler: The Symphonies*, ed. Reinhard G. Pauly, trans. Vernon and Jutta Wicker (Portland, Ore.: Amadeus Press, 1993), 76–77. Used by permission.

13. Frederick Buechner, *Wishful Thinking: A Theological ABC* (New York: Harper and Row, 1973), 95.

14. Auden, "In Praise of Limestone," *Collected Poems*, 540. Used by permission.

15. Ibid.

16. T. S. Eliot, "Journey of the Magi," *The Complete Poems and Plays* (New York: Harcourt, Brace, & World, 1952), 69. Used by permission.

17. Auden, "In Praise of Limestone," 542. Used by permission.

Other Books from The Pilgrim Press

Sacred Journey

Spiritual Wisdom for Times of Transition

MIKE RIDDELL

This inspiring and challenging book is for anyone who has ever asked, "What now?" or "What will be left of my life when I am gone?" In an engrossing blend of reflection and story, Riddell encourages us to regain our capacity for wonder and to discover the unique gift that only we can bring to the world.

0-8298-1456-6/paper/224 pages/ $16.00

Encounters with the Ever-present God

HOWARD W. ROBERTS

God comes to the world through people. And people today usually react to God's presence in the same manner as people before us. This book explores biblical accounts of how God has come to people and then builds bridges from biblical lives to contemporary lives.

0-8298-1435-3/paper/144 pages/ $12.00

Living the Labyrinth

101 Paths to a Deeper Connection

JILL KIMBERLY HARTWELL GEOFFRION

This resource offers beginners and seasoned labyrinth users a multitude of new ways to approach this sacred tool. The short, devotional-like chapters may be used however the reader chooses because, as Geoffrion tells us, any way we live the labyrinth is the "right" way.

0-8298-1372-1/paper/88 pages/ $16.95

To order these or any other books from The Pilgrim Press call or write to:

THE PILGRIM PRESS
700 Prospect Avenue East
Cleveland, Ohio 44115-1100

Phone orders: 800.537.3394
Fax orders: 216.736.2206
Please include shipping charges of $4.00 for the first book and 75¢ for each additional book. Or order from our Web sites at <www.pilgrimpress.com> and <www.ucpress.com>.

Prices subject to change without notice.